A CLINICIAN'S
GUIDE TO
SYSTEMIC
SEX
THERAPY

A Clinician's Guide to Systemic Sex Therapy

Katherine M. Hertlein
Gerald R. Weeks
Shelley K. Sendak

Routledge
Taylor & Francis Group
New York   London

Routledge
Taylor & Francis Group
270 Madison Avenue
New York, NY 10016

Routledge
Taylor & Francis Group
2 Park Square
Milton Park, Abingdon
Oxon OX14 4RN

© 2009 by Taylor & Francis Group, LLC
Routledge is an imprint of Taylor & Francis Group, an Informa business

Printed in the United States of America on acid-free paper
10 9 8 7 6 5 4 3 2 1

International Standard Book Number-13: 978-0-7890-3823-4 (Softcover) 978-0-7890-3822-7 (Hardcover)

Library of Congress Cataloging-in-Publication Data

Hertlein, Katherine M.
    A clinician's guide to systemic sex therapy / Katherine M. Hertlein, Gerald R. Weeks, Shelley K. Sendak.
        p. ; cm.
    Includes bibliographical references and index.
    ISBN 978-0-7890-3822-7 (hardback : alk. paper) -- ISBN 978-0-7890-3823-4 (pbk. : alk. paper)
        1. Sex therapy. I. Weeks, Gerald R., 1948- II. Sendak, Shelley K. III. Title.
    [DNLM: 1. Couples Therapy--methods. 2. Marital Therapy--methods. 3. Sexual Dysfunction, Physiological--therapy. 4. Sexual Dysfunctions, Psychological--therapy. WM 430.5.M3 H574c 2009]

RC557.H47 2009
616.89'1562--dc22   2008034967

Visit the Taylor & Francis Web site at
http://www.taylorandfrancis.com

and the Routledge Web site at
http://www.routledge.com

To Eric, with love.

—KMH

To Nancy, for the love you bring to my life.

—GW

To Patricia, whom I love completely.

—SKS

Contents

SECTION II   Practice Issues and Resources for Sex Therapy

Acknowledgments

This book would not be possible without several key individuals. First, we extend grateful appreciation to Dr. Thorana Nelson for her invitation for this book. She is a wonderful series editor—knowledgeable and available—and she guided us through this process. We also want to extend a thank you to Dr. Terry Trepper and his work in this field. He is a great source of motivation and a hard worker, and we are lucky to have someone so wonderful to guide us on this journey. It is also very important to acknowledge the work of Dr. Gerald Weeks. This book is based on his approach to sex therapy, which he has developed over many years and was generous enough to share with his students, colleagues, and clients. We thank him for this opportunity to share his approach with others and are inspired by his warm personality and dedication to the field.

Another key player is Dr. Nancy Gambescia. She did much writing with Dr. Weeks on this model and helped to refine the approach through her scholarship and application of the approach to her cases. We would also like to acknowledge the work of Dr. Amy Ellwood on this book. Dr. Ellwood served as a reviewer for the chapters on assessment and treatment and assisted us in providing a more descriptive discussion for beginning therapists in key areas. We thank the staff at both Haworth Press and Taylor & Francis for their support of this project, specifically the work of George Zimmar, Fred Coppersmith, and Marta Moldvai. They continually provided valuable guidance and direction in the preparation of this manuscript and guided us through the pragmatic issues related to publication. Finally, we would like to acknowledge the work of the graduate assistants who helped in the preparation of this book, including Armeda Stevenson, Blendine P. Hawkins, Lisa Schapiro, and Lindsay Haywood. We could not have done it without you!

About the Authors

Katherine M. Hertlein, PhD, is an assistant professor in the Department of Marriage and Family Therapy at the University of Nevada, Las Vegas. She is a licensed marriage and family therapist and an AAMFT-approved supervisor. She received her master's degree in marriage and family therapy from Purdue University, Calumet, and her PhD in marriage and family therapy from Virginia Tech. She has published in several academic journals related to couple and family therapy, including the *Journal of Marital and Family Therapy, The Family Journal,* and the *Journal of Couple and Relationship Therapy.* She serves as reviewer for several journals, as a coeditor for a book on therapy interventions for couples and families, and as a coeditor on a book for the clinical treatment of infidelity. Her areas of interest include infidelity treatment, research methodology and measurement, and training in marriage and family therapy.

Gerald R. Weeks, PhD, is professor and chair of the Department of Marriage and Family Therapy at the University of Nevada, Las Vegas. He is a licensed psychologist, fellow, approved-supervisor, and clinical member of the American Association of Marriage and Family Therapy, and he is board certified by the American Board of Professional Psychology and the American Board of Sexology. He has published 18 books, including the major contemporary texts in the fields of sex, marital, and family therapy. Dr. Weeks is the past president of the American Board of Family Psychology and has lectured extensively throughout North America and Europe on sex, couple, and psychotherapy. Dr. Weeks has close to 30 years of experience in practicing and supervising sex, couple, and family therapy.

Shelley K. Sendak holds a PhD in sociology and a certificate in clinical sexology from the American Academy of Clinical Sexology. She frequently teaches courses in women's studies, women's sexuality, and sexual minority health. Dr. Sendak's areas of interest include visual sociology, the impact of sociocultural understandings of sexuality on sexual well-being and satisfaction, and applied research in mental health. She has published a women's studies textbook and several works on homoerotica and her visual essays have appeared in a variety of academic publications, including text-books in social work, gerontology, family studies, and social inequality.

Section I

Conducting Sex Therapy Step by Step From an Intersystems Approach

1

The Intersystems Approach to Sex Therapy

Introduction

The purpose of this book is to provide the reader with an integrative and comprehensive theory in guiding his or her clinical practice. Most of this text is pragmatically oriented. We inform the reader how to go about diagnosing and treating, with many resources such as tables, graphs, flow charts, and implementation strategies. The use of this information needs to be guided by a theory that can be translated into practice. The Intersystems approach that we have developed gives the clinician this guide.

Couple Therapy, Sex Therapy, and the Intersystems Approach

Theory and Integration in Couple Therapy

Any new development in couple therapy can be imported into sex therapy, as we have demonstrated in several earlier texts (Weeks & Gambescia, 2000; 2002). We also believe that it is absolutely essential that the fields of couple and sex therapy be fully integrated theoretically and pragmatically. The field of couple therapy has experienced a significant evolution over the last several decades, particularly in terms of its theoretical development (Gurman & Fraenkel, 2002). We consider sex therapy a subset of couple therapy. The earliest theoretical phase of couple therapy was described as "atheoretical" and the cited theories were drawn from the psychoanalytic theories of the time. As the field evolved, the theories used for couple therapy began to incorporate the family therapy models, heavily influenced by the work of Jackson, Satir, Bowen, and Haley (Gurman & Fraenkel, 2002). With the idea that multiple frameworks might or could be combined into one treatment, many books and papers were published in the 1970s and 1980s describing how one might integrate theories (Weeks, 1989, 1994).* Such examples include:

- Duhl and Duhl (1981): integrative therapy focusing on individual process and transactional patterns;
- Duncan and Parks (1988): integrating behavioral and strategic therapies; and
- Hatcher (1978): integrating family therapy and gestalt therapies.

Over time, couple therapy has shifted from what Olson described as a field without a strong theoretical base (as cited in Gurman & Fraenkel, 2002) to its present state, described as theoretical refinement and integration (Gurman & Fraenkel, 2002).

The shift toward integration in couple therapy and sex therapy is encapsulated in the Intersystems approach. The Intersystems approach was initially developed by Gerald Weeks (1986), who used the term "intersystems" to describe how individual and systems theories interact in our lives. In its application to couple and sex therapy, this theoretically based approach provides a comprehensive perspective in understanding and improving the state of intimate, sexual relationships for clients and for the therapist trying to help them resolve their sexual problems in a larger context than previously undertaken.

The Intersystems framework offers a way to approach couple sex therapy from a dialectical metatheoretical perspective as described by Riegel (1976). At its basis, the Intersystems application of Riegel's dialectics sees a connection between an individual's inner and outer worlds, the intrapsychic processes that impact and are impacted upon by a variety of factors, including interpersonal dynamics, physiology, psychology, culture, and social situation. It incorporates all of these areas to understand and treat sexual problems and represents a true integration of these parts of a couple system.

Moving Toward Theoretical Integration

The Intersystems approach is unique in that it is a truly integrative perspective. Many theories and frameworks that purport to be integrative are

---

* A useful review article concerning the efforts to integrate family therapies was published by Case and Robinson (1990).

actually technically eclectic. This differs from integration in that technical eclecticism is composed of several frameworks operating together without a coherent theoretical foundation. This may be because philosophical or metatheoretical concepts are not normally explicated in most approaches to therapy and, in many cases, clinicians are not trained in metatheoretical thinking. As a result, therapists operating from technical eclecticism use a variety of concepts and techniques from different theories based on clinical judgment.

To be truly integrative in therapeutic work, the therapist must consider both foundational constructs (i.e., those that provide a frame of reference for the integration of different theories) and integrative constructs (i.e., those that provide a way to unify different theories) (Van Kaam, 1969). A therapist working from an integrative approach has an articulated theoretical foundation and a clear conceptual framework that informs diagnosis and treatment. As a result, the Intersystems approach is a more thorough, sophisticated, responsible, and ethical approach (Slife & Reber, 2001) than other "integrative" therapies.

In addition to the lack of comprehensive theoretical integration in the practice of couple and sex therapy, there is also a lack of integration in the professional fields of sex therapy and couple therapy. For example, many professional organizations in the field of marriage and family therapy have overlapping interests but operate in isolation of one another. The American Association for Marriage and Family Therapy (AAMFT) and the American Counseling Association (ACA) have established standards for the practice of couple therapy, yet there is little emphasis on sex therapy training for students as outlined in their training standards (CACREP, 2001; COAMFTE, 2002). Also, although the American Association of Sexuality Educators, Counselors, and Therapists (AASECT) has established educational and supervisory standards for certification in sex therapy, very little training in couple or family therapy is required to become a certified sex therapist. Second, there has been separation or fragmentation of these two fields historically at the theoretical level. Sex therapy, marital therapy, and family therapy have had different historical theoretical trajectories. The texts in these fields show very little confluence or mixing of approaches. Finally, the literature in the field frequently does not contain elements of theory. Given the evidence, it is not surprising that the practicing clinicians are also plagued by an inability to be truly integrative because of the lack of a theory to guide their work.

The Intersystems model is the result of over 20 years of refinement through scholarly thought and clinical practice. Its development began after Weeks's (1977) initial writings on the dialectical approach to couple therapy. Weeks and Hof (1987) published the first book on the integration of sex and marital therapy, which moved the field of sex therapy away from a strictly individual perspective toward a systems perspective. Subsequently, Weeks published several books demonstrating the practicality of the Intersystems approach with a variety of clinical problems. Weeks and Hof (1994), for example, outlined the approach and demonstrated how it could be used in couple therapy in general, especially in cases of lack of desire. Weeks and Gambescia (2000, 2002) have also written several books utilizing the approach in the treatment of erectile dysfunction, hypoactive sexual desire, and infidelity.

As couple therapy moves more deeply into Gurman and Fraenkel's (2002) refinement/integration phase, couple therapists should continue to become clearer regarding the theories informing their practice. Further, clarity in one's epistemology results in an appropriate application of systemic frameworks and results in integrative treatment (L'Abate, 2007). Therapists must understand what each theory or construct contributes to their overall treatment plan. The Intersystems approach does exactly that without advocating for one particular theory or model of couple therapy. It helps therapists to identify an epistemology or philosophy from which they base their assumptions about people and change, and to articulate specifically how each of the theories selected within their clinical work is consistent with their overarching approach to treatment.

Intersystems Theory and Application

The Intersystems sex therapy paradigm is informed by two components: Sternberg's triangular theory of love (1986) and the theory of interaction (Strong & Claiborn, 1982). These frameworks consistently attend to the emotions, cognitions, and behaviors of the couple. They address the couple's issues, including those related to sexuality, and operate effectively together to create a cohesive paradigm rather than a series of isolated and disconnected models of therapy.

Sternberg (1986), a social psychologist, developed a triangular theory of love discussing three components: commitment, intimacy, and passion. He asserted that each of these components interfaced with one another in relationships. Although some therapists may attend to only one of the three sides of the triangle, we believe it is necessary to attend to all three, shifting emphasis as the case warrants. Focusing on each of these elements ensures that the etiology of the couple's problem as well as the particular sexual problem is addressed from an integrative perspective.

Strong and Claiborn's (1982) theory of interaction addresses the idea that there are both intrapsychic (the way in which each partner attributes the communications of the other) and interactional (the way in which communication is completed within the couple) components active in all relationships. The Intersystems approach adopts this paradigm and incorporates both of these components into the understanding of what sexual difficulties mean to the couple and how each partner understands his or her role in communicating about sexuality and intimacy.

Intrapsychic Components

The intrapsychic components used within the Intersystems approach include interpretation, definition, and prediction. Interpretation (meaning that is ascribed to an event, behavior, or problem) refers to the extent to which one interprets his or her partner's behavior inaccurately. For example, a partner who suffers from hypoactive sexual desire disorder may have a partner who interprets this behavior as unloving and uncaring. The partner may interpret the behavior as an intentional withholding of sex out of anger or some other negative feeling. This attribution, though incorrect, will be that which underlines the partner's future behavior and shapes his or her views about the partner and the relationship.

Definition (the reciprocal arrangement of how the relationship defines each partner and how each partner defines the relationship) can infiltrate the couple's view of the relationship without awareness, influencing cognitions, affect, and behavior. For instance, someone with more sexual experience might have different expectations of what constitutes "a lot" of sex or what is included in "kinky" sex than his or her partner. If this expectation is articulated, partners can come to some agreement on the frequency and types of behaviors that will constitute part of their relationship. If these expectations are not articulated or are unconscious, communication problems may develop between the couple. It then becomes incumbent upon the therapist to help the couple address the unspoken expectations. In another case, one partner may define the relationship as highly sexual while the other might define the relationship as highly romantic. The partners are not in agreement about how the relationship is to be defined sexually. They have different definitions of their relationship and therapists can assist them in obtaining clarity about (1) the progression of the relationship, and (2) the definition of terms used without conscious understanding of their implications.

Prediction addresses the notion that, to some degree, human beings have a tendency to try to predict each other's behaviors or thoughts or a particular outcome. Frequently, intimate partners believe that, once they know their partner well, they can predict the partner's behavior. Further, we tend to make positive predictions, such as that the other person is loving, caring, generous, sensitive, wanting to meet our needs, etc. When the other person does not respond as expected or predicted, it can raise questions about the fundamental nature of the relationship. For example, a client, upon finding her partner using pornography, stated, "I thought my partner had sexual thoughts about me and only me. Now that I know it isn't true, I don't know who this person is." The fact that one prediction turned out to be false now calls into question all other predictions about the partner. Sex therapists frequently see faulty prediction as it impacts homework completion. The therapist may begin the treatment with an assignment such as sensate focus exercises, thinking it an easy assignment with which the couple will readily comply. The clients, on the other hand, do not complete homework, predicting (consciously or not) that any attempt to connect physically will result in anger, disappointment, a sense of failure, or any other negative feeling associated with sexual interaction in the past.

Interactional Components

The interactional components include congruence, interdependence, and attributional strategy. Congruence refers to the degree to which couples share or agree on how events are defined. For example, a husband may consider his wife's online chatting with other men as a form of infidelity, but the wife does not. The definition of the event may be incongruent relationally because, in the husband's definition, the wife is cheating, but in her mind she is having a friendly chat. The couple can also agree that they define infidelity differently, thus being congruent in their assessment of incongruency. They still face the dilemma of how they are both acting in accordance with their various and conflicting definitions of fidelity. Further, in many cases of hypoactive sexual desire disorder, one partner may believe that the couple is having sex often, but the other partner disagrees. The partner with the lower level of desire perceives that he or she is having sex more frequently than claimed by the partner who wants sex more frequently. The therapist will need to help the couple understand whether they have congruent definitions of salient behaviors and then help them reach a consensus.

Interdependence includes partner perceptions of the other's ability to meet emotional and sexual needs and the extent to which partners believe they can depend on each other. For example, an individual may believe that he is meeting his partner's sexual needs, but the partner is desperate to explore sex with someone else, believing that satisfaction can only come from another person. This couple demonstrates a low level of interdependence. Couples with high levels of interdependence typically proceed through treatment more quickly than couples with low levels. If the partners are highly interdependent, they typically will want to continue to fulfill each other's needs in hopes that the reciprocity of need fulfillment will continue unabated. Those who are less interdependent may be tentative about the continuation of the relationship and therefore less willing to change for the sake of the other or the relationship. When a therapist is working with couples with lower levels of interdependence, it may be helpful to focus on a discussion of commitment. A common example of interdependence can be found in the desire for differing sexual activities. A man may wish to have oral sex, but his partner refuses because she feels it is perverted or disgusting.*

Attributional strategy is the manner in which partners ascribe meaning to an event, and a couple can define relationship events in either a linear or circular fashion. In a linear attribution strategy, a partner attributes his spouse's behavior directly (effect) to a specific stimulus (cause). A husband, for instance, might report that his wife "makes" him angry when she nags him about household chores. Most couples will display linear attributional strategies and therapists are wise to point out quickly the circular nature of the couple's dynamics. Circular attribution strategies are those where partners examine the impact of their behavior on the other in a reciprocal or interlocking way. The partners are able to comprehend that they each affect the other and are affected by the other. The thinking is not linear, but rather circular and reciprocal (systemic).

Reframing is the primary technique sex therapists can use to help the couple move from linear and blaming statements to a more circular and

---

* In our experience, it is often the woman who wishes to receive oral sex, but the other partner states that it is distasteful, disgusting, unpleasant, and unclean.

positive view of their dynamics.* For example, Rachael and Mike came to therapy because Rachel often had difficulty reaching orgasm during intercourse. She claimed the reason was because Mike sometimes lost his erection. She did not see that she had a role in her inability to reach orgasm; initially, she believed only he was to be blamed. Rachael typically needed about 20 minutes of stimulation to climax, but she started to become frustrated after about 10 minutes of intercourse if she had not yet reached orgasm. Prior to sex, she would tell Mike that he needed to thrust faster, what position she needed, that she wanted intercourse for a long time, and that he needed to keep a good erection throughout. Mike tried his best to please her, but he was so anxious about performing well that it made keeping an erection difficult. She frequently told him he was doing something wrong during intercourse, making matters worse for Mike's ability to maintain an erection.

The therapist might address the attribution by pointing out how much each liked sex and how clear it was that each one wanted to please the other. However, Rachel's wish to reach orgasm more quickly to make Mike's life easier and Mike's desperate concern with Rachel's pleasure combined to create escalating anxiety on *both* sides. Mike's anxiety stemmed from sensing Rachel's pressure. This anxiety made it more difficult for her to reach orgasm and more difficult for him to maintain an erection. In addition to highlighting the circular nature of the problem, some psychoeducation on male and female sexuality and different techniques to enhance Rachel's pleasure (thereby opening up other options for her orgasm) reduced the pressure on their relationship and changed their sexual patterns.

Understanding Etiology and Treatment
Within the Intersystems Approach

The Intersystems approach directs our attention to several aspects of the "system." Each part of the system is given equal attention in terms of assessment. Once the clinician has examined each of these aspects of the system, a treatment plan can be constructed that attends to each of the aspects of the system requiring intervention. This framework has

---

* Weeks and Treat (2001) discuss reframing in its application to couple and sexual problems at length. Weeks and Gambescia (2002) also discuss the use of reframing in treating hypoactive sexual desire.

five components: individual, biological, and medical; individual and psychological; dyadic relationship; family of origin; and society, culture, history, and religion. Each of these five parts of the system is examined in terms of the part it plays in the creation of the sexual problem. The relevant parts are then incorporated into a comprehensive treatment plan.

Individual and Biological

Each person's biology is different. Therefore, one needs to consider the influence of each individual's health status and medical concerns on the relationship and its connection with the individual's sexual problems. For example, in the treatment of erectile dysfunction, therapists are well advised to consider any medical problems or hormonal issues potentially contributing to the dysfunction. Certain psychological disorders with biological components such as bipolar disorder may also contribute to problems experienced by a couple. In addition, certain medications can also impact sexual function. Selective serotonin reuptake inhibitors (SSRIs) and atypical SSRIs (particularly Paxil, Remeron, and Effexor) have significant sexual side effects, including diminished libido and delayed or absent orgasm.[*] If a therapist develops a hypothesis that medications might be impacting sexual functioning, the client should contact an appropriate physician and discuss this issue.

A typical case involved a therapist seeing a couple who had been married for 18 years. The presenting problem was that the wife was experiencing orgasm with intercourse about 50% of the time and was always orgasmic in other cases where she wanted to be. The therapist, in conducting a typical assessment, discovered that the wife's father had passed away recently. Although the therapist assumed that the wife was depressed, the therapist did not associate the depression medications with having any impact on the couple's sexual functioning. As a result, the interventions that were tried were unsuccessful, leading to greater frustration for the couple, reducing orgasm for the wife, and complicating the sexual problem already occurring.

---

[*] See Chapter 7 for a brief listing of such medications as well as Seagraves and Balon (2005).

Individual and Psychological

The Intersystems approach points to the importance of taking a wide view of the aspects involved in an individual's psychological makeup. The approach to this component includes (but is not limited to) the following:

- personality (including personality disorders);
- psychopathology;
- intelligence;
- temperament;
- developmental stages and deficits;
- attitudes;
- values; and
- defense mechanisms.

An individual's psychological composition influences what one understands about sexuality and how to express it. There may be a history of depression, other psychological issues, or covert messages about sexuality that are impacting the current relationship. For example, a person experiencing depression may not feel desire to engage in sexual activity, particularly if the depression is related to the relationship. A person's sexual experience may also have been acquired in a way that elicits guilt about particular sexual activities, thus inhibiting desire. Therapists can gather information about a client's psychological composition by taking an adequate history and utilizing the history-taking methods (see Chapters 2 and 8).

Dyadic/Couple Relationship

Though it is important to assess each individual's behavioral patterns, the Intersystems approach also addresses how these individual behaviors manifest as interlocking patterns within the couple. For almost every couple in sex therapy, there are couple factors that contribute to and maintain the sexual dysfunction. These couple issues include (but are not limited to):

- defining the relationship in an incongruent way;
- making negative attributions about each other;
- regulation of intimacy;
- fears (of dependency, intimacy, etc.);
- communication;

- dealing with conscious and unconscious expectations; and
- conflict management.

While acknowledging the contributions of each individual to the couple, the Intersystems approach defines the client as the relationship, or the "space in between" the partners (A. Krueger, personal communication, 2007). In other words, the focus is on the couple's dynamics and how these dynamics may contribute to sexual problems. Consider the case of Martha and Jack, who had been married about 30 years when they entered therapy for a sexual problem. Martha did most of the talking in the session and wanted to set the agenda. Considering how the couple's behavior in a session is often isomorphic with how they behave at home, the therapist started to explore how they communicate. Jack said he thought their communication was fine, but Martha said Jack never said much, was not assertive or expressive of his needs, and never expressed any statements of feeling. Due to Jack's lack of communication, Martha had withdrawn sexually and Jack had learned not to respond to any sexual need. A traditionally trained sex therapist would have probably focused on their lack of sexual communication and given the couple instructions on how to better communicate about sensual and sexual needs.

An Intersystems therapist would explore Jack's lack of communication from his early years, his current lack of communication, and Martha's role in allowing this pattern to continue for so long. The therapist first explored the family of origin and found that his parents were verbally abusive to each other and toward Jack. He learned not to speak because he would be viewed as a troublemaker; he stayed away from home as much as possible in his youth. The therapist surmised that he was seeking a partner who would be quiet, nonconfrontational, and avoid conflict. Some exploration with Jack confirmed that this was his unconscious motivation for marriage to Martha. On the other hand, Martha saw the good in Jack and thought he would open up after marriage. Contributing to the dynamics, Martha had a history of caretaking in her family. The therapist recognized her need for caretaking and confirmed Martha's desire to rescue Jack.

In this case example, the therapist redirected much of the initial therapy toward couple dynamics and family-of-origin issues rather than the sexual issue that they initially presented. This is critical to the Intersystems approach: Frequently, the therapist must persuade the couple that the "real" or underlying problem to their sexual problem is to be found in their relationship. Couple therapy can only proceed successfully with a couple such as this after a convincing argument can be made for doing couple work. The couple must be fully convinced and committed to doing the couple work prior to focusing on the sexual issue.

In short, the sex therapist must be a well-trained couple therapist who knows how to assess issues that impact sexuality and treat the couple relationship. The traditional approach of exclusively treating sexual problems in isolation and behaviorally, which has been the norm in the past, will likely be met with resistance and eventually fail. From a systemic perspective, the sexual problem is a symptom of a dysfunctional relationship and will resolve with help if the couple problem is resolved.

Family of Origin

One place where people learn about relationships and sexuality is in their families of origin. Messages distributed about sexuality within one's family can be (1) covert, (2) overt, (3) internalized, and/or (4) expressed in one's relationships. When sexuality in families is not openly discussed, children in these families may interpret this behavior to mean that sexuality is inherently "bad" and that expression of it should be minimized. As these children grow into adulthood, they may struggle with their emerging sexuality and tell themselves that they are "bad" for having such feelings. This impacts their self-esteem and, inevitably, their relationships.

Some parents are overt in their condemnation of sexual behavior, again resulting in internal struggles for their children as they grow into adulthood and develop intimate relationships. Research demonstrates that children from dysfunctional families (with or without sexual abuse) are more likely to develop sexual dysfunctions such as hypoactive sexual desire disorder (Kinzl, Mangwerth, Traweger, & Biebel, 1996; Kinzl, Traweger, & Biebel, 1995). Sex therapists are wise to obtain information about family history via a relationship/sexual genogram (genograms specific to sexuality and how to obtain them are discussed in detail in Chapter 3).

Pat and Vincent entered therapy with an unusual presentation. Vincent claimed that Pat had always had too high a sex drive and after several years of marriage he had given up on trying to fulfill her sexual needs. If the therapist had accepted this presentation, then the strategy might have been to decrease her sexual drive and increase his. After a few sessions, the therapist had learned that Pat had been sexually abused by her father, but never sought any help. Although the typical pattern for a sexually abused woman is to present with diminished sex drive, she fell into the opposite category, as some women do. Prior to marriage, the couple was hypersexual and Vincent enjoyed the sex. On their wedding night, Vincent refused to have sex with her, started finding fault with her behavior, and brought up her sexual past in a highly negative way. Pat felt he was suggesting that she was a slut. This behavior continued throughout an extended honeymoon trip, with Pat reporting the honeymoon made up some of the worst days of her life.

Once they settled into their lives, Vincent demonstrated little sexual interest. Pat was always initiating sex. The therapist learned that Vincent was having emotional affairs with a number of women. He would spend hours on the phone or text messaging multiple women he knew. He appeared to be using these other relationships as a way to distance from Pat emotionally. Exploration of his family of origin showed that he had an overbearing, smothering mother. Vincent was afraid that Pat might take on the same role if he allowed her to do so. Thus, he found ways to distance himself and justified it by blaming Pat for her sexual history of acting out prior to marriage and finding fault with her. No matter what she did, it was never good enough. The therapist revealed the couple's current pattern of behavior and linked it to their family of origin. The initial phase of therapy was directed toward helping Pat understand the consequences of her sexual abuse and working through it. For Vincent, the work was more difficult. He could see the link intellectually, but had trouble letting go of his self-protective behavior of distancing himself.

Society, Culture, History, and Religion

The last component is the couple's societal and cultural environment and its effect on their relationship. Everything in the environment that can affect the ability to form a healthy sexual relationship, including beliefs, customs, and values around sexuality and sexual expression, is part of an individual's and couple's sociocultural environment. For example, some cultures or subgroups may prohibit masturbation, but other cultures have greater sexual permissiveness. This becomes important in treatment planning, where some clients may be opposed to sexual self-exploration. Clients also feel the pressure of the external environment, which complicates their sexual problem. For example, one couple struggling with hypoactive sexual desire disorder reported how difficult their honeymoon was because they were surrounded by other couples who were, presumably, having sex while they were not, and this led to an argument on the trip. Over time, values about sexual behaviors such as masturbation, different positions, oral sex, premarital sex, anal sex, and so on have changed significantly. As norms change, couples should work to understand the extent to which culture and contemporary society have played into their decision-making, values, and behaviors as a couple.

Terrance represents one case in which cultural and societal background played a key factor. He came to therapy individually because, every time he tried to have sex, he experienced back pain and would lose his erection. The therapist quickly learned that he always used the missionary position and never considered or even thought of another position that might take the stress off his back. The obvious solution was to suggest that he try the male-on-bottom position. However, the therapist realized that something must have prevented him from realizing the obvious. The therapist discovered that he and his wife were fundamentalist Christians. They grew up in the Bible belt and religion was a central part of their lives. The therapist needed to understand Terrance's religious beliefs about sex in order to challenge them. Basically, he believed that sex was only proper after marriage and otherwise he was reared in a sexual vacuum. He had heard of the missionary position and assumed that it was the only "proper" position.

The therapist gently challenged this belief as an assumption and asked if he knew of any biblical verse that prescribed a particular sexual position. He could not think of any. The therapist asked whether God had given man the ability to have sex in other positions, to which Terrance answered that He must have. At this point, Terrance spontaneously said that God must want man to try different positions and he had only been using one. The therapist could now suggest that he try the female-on-top position with his wife to see if that would alleviate his back pain. However, he would need to discuss this with his wife first and talk about the religious insight he had experienced. With all these things done, Terrance experienced a "miracle cure" within the first week.

Conclusion

In sum, the Intersystems approach guides the clinician in integrating the individual, interactional, transgenerational, and other sociocultural factors that may be affecting sexual functioning. Integration begins with the assessment phase leading to a case formulation (described fully in Chapter 4) and then continues throughout therapy. The therapist may shift back and forth between or among the different elements of the Intersystems approach in a flexible and fluid way that best serves the clients' needs.

Therapists are usually trained in several approaches nested within one or two modalities, and therapists using this approach should be knowledge-able in the areas of couple and family therapy, sex therapy, and individual therapy. This fact makes mastery of the Intersystems treatment approach one of the most ambitious and challenging for any therapist. The challenge is to continue learning in order to master as many approaches to therapy as possible within as many modalities as possible. The Intersystems approach renders a way to conduct a comprehensive assessment and provide a flex-ible treatment approach designed for each unique couple. Because we believe that every couple is different, rather than making them fit one spe-cific modality, we fit them to an all-encompassing approach, thereby giv-ing each couple individualized treatment.

2

Assessment Within the Intersystems Approach*

Introduction

Assessment in sex therapy is a critical and continuous part of the therapeutic process. Information gathered early in the assessment process frequently establishes a diagnosis, leads to case formulation or conceptualization, and provides the basis for treatment planning. With any assessment, it is important to determine:

- current baseline;
- optimal sexual functioning (the couple's ideal sex life at the end of treatment);
- sexual desire;
- sexual satisfaction;
- level of distress experienced because of the sexual problem; and
- the problem's impact on intimate relationships.

As treatment continues, the use of assessments should be expanded to include treatment monitoring (including decisions in who participates in treatment), the structure of the sessions, and the interventions planned. Finally, clinicians can use assessments at the end of the therapeutic process to determine treatment outcome more precisely. For sex therapists, most assessment of sexual problems will rely upon the client report, with information coming in a variety of formats including self-report, inventories, structured interviews, event logs, and client diaries.

---

* Written with Amy Ellwood.

The Biphasic Assessment Process

The Intersystems assessment process can be conceptualized in two phases. The first phase is to gain general information about the presenting problem. The first phase is to gain general information about the presenting problem. Assuming the presenting problem is sexual the therapist should ask about the sexual functioning within the relationship, including solo sex or self with oneself. The therapist then moves to the second phase of expanding the context of the assessment to include questions about the couple's overall relationship and other broader contextual material. The first phase is to gain general information about the clients, including general information on health history, sexuality, and the couple relationship. In the first phase, the therapist may begin by asking about the nature of the sexual problem. However, many couples do not want to admit they have a problem or do not recognize that a problem is a problem. Thus, the next question is intended to draw out any other sexual problems. The therapist says, "Are you saying that you don't have a problem with [too little desire, problems getting or keeping an erection, having difficulty ejaculating, difficulty reaching orgasm, pain with intercourse, disagreements about the use of pornography, too little foreplay, partner choosing an inconvenient time, one partner wanting to do things the other does not, and so on]?"

The second phase is to gain more detailed information about the specific problems, their etiologies, and how the sexual difficulties are impacting the individual and interpersonal levels. It involves asking more general questions about each of the sexual problems that has been identified and the relationship. Because of space limitations, we are not including relationship assessment, except in a few cases. These specific questions are essential, but certainly not all inclusive or exhaustive of the information that needs to be gathered. Additionally, we are including only the classical or most common sexual problems and not some of the less frequently presented or newly developed diagnoses. Basically, the therapist is going through a checklist of possible sexual difficulties in order to rule them out. The therapist should be sure to ask about:

- *Any physical illnesses or chronic medical conditions.* The therapist should always inquire about medications, especially psychotropic medications that may have adverse sexual side effects (Seagraves & Balon, 2003).
- *The overall couple relationship.* The therapist wants to get a picture of how the couple perceives strengths and problems in their relationship (Weeks & Treat, 1992). The therapist will also want to get a picture of some of the most common of couple problems, such as anger, conflict,

roles, and other aspects of intimacy described elsewhere in this volume, and see whether the couple thinks there is a relationship between their sexual problems and relationship problems. Couples that do not see how the two are linked will need some work to make these connections in order for them to believe the therapist is working on the right issues.

- *The level of affection in their relationship.* In many sex therapy cases, affection is viewed as a prelude to sex and avoided. The therapist needs to get a list of the couple's behaviors that they define as affectionate and determine whether they see this only as a precursor to sex.
- *The level of sensuality in their relationship.* Sensuality is giving each other physical pleasure without becoming sexual.
- *The level of communication.* How do they talk to each other about sex? Can they ask for what they want to give and get from each other during a sensual and sexual encounter?
- *Whether there is anything else the therapist needs to know.* Couples may have other significant problems they do not want to discuss other than the sexual problem. For example, an alcoholic man may not want to discuss his drinking, but just focus on his erectile problems.

Taking a Sex History

Since the inception of the study of sexuality, several coding systems have been devised to take an individual's sexual history. The first notable system was developed by American biologist Alfred Kinsey. He developed a way to record all of a person's sexual experiences, no matter how extensive, on a single sheet of paper. His coding system was designed in such a way that anyone else who looked at the coding sheet would not be able to tell what the topic area was about or who the interviewee was, in order to protect the confidentiality of his respondents.

Since the development of Kinsey's coding system, many sex therapists have developed their own questionnaires, often combining some of Hirschfeld's and Kinsey's questions with new ones of their own. For example, Hartman and Fithian (1972) addressed how one might take a sexual history in their book, *Treatment of Sexual Dysfunction: A Bio-Psycho-Social Approach.* Wardell Pomeroy, a close associate of Kinsey, co-wrote *Taking a Sex History—Interviewing and Coding* based on the Kinsey assessment techniques.

The key to providing clients with meaningful answers to their problems lies in asking the right questions. The main objective in taking a sex history is to gain an accurate representation of a client's sexual history and current behavior in order to screen for the presence of sexual problems, to provide insight into possible etiology, and to indicate the treatment most likely to be efficacious. However, there is no standardized interview, such as the Diagnostic Interview Schedule (Compton & Cottier, 2004), for sexual disorders, so clinicians are left to create their own.

Although the content in a sexual history varies depending on its author, the most basic information that therapists will typically find useful includes personal demographic information, relationship status and history, sexual experiences with past and current partners, previous sexual violence or abuse, and any previous diagnosis of sexual dysfunctions or sexually transmitted infections. Much of the general information can be obtained on intake forms, such as those provided at the end of this chapter, leaving the more detailed questions for a clinical interview. Weeks and Gambescia (2000; 2002) have incorporated several other dimensions into sexual history taking. Using the Intersystems approach, the techniques include an assessment of individual factors (such as medical conditions and psychological disorders), the ability to fantasize, an appraisal of any cognitive distortions (i.e., misconceptions about sex), and the use of the sexual genogram and other related focused genograms.

A variety of things are assessed when a sex history is taken. In some cases, one aspect of a sex history can be an attempt to identify or uncover the presence of other *DSM-IV-TR* disorders in cases where there is a sexual problem.* The clinician might start by posing questions around the differential diagnosis in some related areas as well as determining whether the symptoms are organic, psychogenic, or secondary to a psychological disorder. Specific questions to make this determination might include focus on immediate or historical psychological, social, environmental, and relational factors in the etiology of the sexual problem.

All sexual histories seem to involve some of the same basic content. These include personal background, sexual education, masturbation and sexual fantasies, sexual relationship with past and current partners, marital history, use of contraceptive methods, history of involvement in group sex, involvement with any sexual violence, solicitation of sexual services, a history of any diagnosed sexual dysfunctions, and an assessment

---

* In some histories, the assessment of the presence of a *DSM-IV-TR* disorder goes beyond whether the *DSM* disorder is classified as a sexual dysfunction. For example, in some cases, Axis II disorders, such as personality disorders, may in fact contribute to the development and maintenance of a sexual dysfunction (see, for example, Weeks & Gambescia, 2002) and therefore should be included in taking sexual history.

of reactions to erotic materials as well as use of erotic materials in one's sexual life. Wincze and Carey (2001) acknowledge that interview structure will vary based on the client, but that, in general, it includes information about childhood (family structure, social status, abuse), adolescence (relationships, self-esteem, menarche in women, substance use), adult life (self-esteem, relationships, sexual experiences), and current sexual functioning (recent changes in sexual functioning flexibility in attitudes, extradyadic relationship, likes and dislikes in sexual behavior). Specific assessment foci related to each category are detailed in Table 2.1.

TABLE 2.1   Typical Sexual History Areas of Assessment

Category	Areas of focus
Individual history	
Personal background	Sex
	Age
	Level of education
	Employment
	Relationship with parents
	Social relationships (siblings, other relatives, friends)
	Marital/relationship status
	Parenthood (number of children, quality of relationships)
	Religious commitment
	Moral values
	Interests and hobbies
	Sports activities
	Psychological disorders
Mental state	Feel depressed or anxious?
	More irritable recently?
	Crying lately?
	Difficulty in getting to sleep?
	Waking in the early hours of the morning?
	Poor appetite at present?
	Changes in weight recently?
	Has your sexual drive been reduced recently?
	Do you have any special fears or phobias?
	Have you ever heard voices or noises that you think other people cannot or have not heard?
	Is your concentration good?

(continued)

TABLE 2.1   Typical Sexual History Areas of Assessment (continued)

Category	Areas of focus
	Is your memory reasonable for your age?
Medical history	Any hospitalizations? When? For what?
	Are you taking any medications? If yes, what? What dosages?
	Illnesses?
	How much do you drink?
	How many cigarettes do you smoke a day?
Interpersonal history	
Family-of-origin factors	What were the ideas communicated to you by your family about sex?
	How did your family communicate affection?
	Family structure?
	Messages about sex?
	Relationship with siblings?
	History of mental illness within the family?
Marital history (if any history)	When? Reason for ending of relationship? Sexual satisfaction?
	How long have you been married to your present partner?
	How long (if at all) did you live together before marriage?
	How many children do you have in the present marriage?
	Have you at any time separated from your present spouse?
	Have you been married before? Please give details, reasons for ending the relationship, number and ages of children, and who is now looking after them.
	Have you or your partner ever had a pregnancy terminated (aborted) for any reason?
	Have you had any infertility problems?
Couple factors	Are the sexual values shared?
	What is the structure of your relationship?
	What is the definition of intimacy? Do you talk about sex? Do you look at one another in the eyes when having sex?
	What is communication like within the relationship?
	How is conflict managed in the relationship?
	How do you spend your leisure time as a couple?
Sex education	Which sexual information was received? When? From whom? Under what circumstances?
	What were the meanings associated with sex?

(continued)

TABLE 2.1   Typical Sexual History Areas of Assessment (continued)

Category	Areas of focus
Masturbation, fantasy, and dreams	When? What? How often?
Sexual experience with others	What was your initiation into sex? How was this interpreted?
	Past experiences: When? What? With whom? How often? Heterosexual or homosexual experiences? Sex with close relatives? Sexual satisfaction?
	Experience with current partner: since when?
	Plans for the future? Sexual satisfaction in current relationship?
	Sex outside the primary relationship: with whom? When? Frequency?
Use of contraceptive methods (if at all)	What method? Duration of use? When used?
Group sex experiences	When? How often? Under what circumstances?
Solicitation of sexual services	Paying for services? Being paid for services? Where? When? Frequency? Under what circumstances?
Sexual violence	Victim and/or perpetrator? How often? When? Where? Who? Under what circumstances?
Erotic responses	How? When? To what?
Sexual problems and dysfunctions	Which? When? Where? Under what circumstances?
Precipitating factors	Medical–physiological changes
	Acute stress
	Crisis in relationship
Coping mechanisms	Fun, positive view of sex
	Ability to reframe positively
	Ability to escape together into fantasy and/or to use sexuality as an escape
	How creative are you?

The relationship or context in which the sexual problem is embedded is also important to evaluate. In some cases, the sexual problems are created or maintained by the relationship. Risk factors—including anger or resentment, fear of intimacy, particular conflict management styles, and power struggles (Metz & Epstein, 2002; Weeks & Gambescia, 2000; 2002)—can sometimes predispose a couple to sexual problems. For example, an overriding negative emotion (such as anger) would probably contribute to negative emotions about the relationship and thus result in sexual impairment. As negative incidents build on top of each other, the relationship becomes a place where the climate is no longer ripe for sexual activity. The interactions in these relationships are based on power and control. This is another type of dynamic that impedes healthy sexual behavior. For example, some clients experiencing lack of sexual desire attribute that fact to power imbalances in the relationship, acknowledging that withholding sex gives them at least some power in the relationship (Weeks & Gambescia, 2002).

Like any other assessment method, interviewing the client has a series of advantages and disadvantages. According to Bancroft (1990), some advantages of interviewing in the assessment of sexual problems include the therapist's ability to check with the client about his or her understanding of the problem as well as the development of rapport in a relatively safe environment. Disadvantages include the time involved in conducting a proper interview, the potential for bias in the manner in which questions are asked or interpreted, and the lack of anonymity of the client. Clients may also feel that extensive assessments are unnecessary and want to move prematurely to treatment.

Guidelines in Taking Sexual History

Understand One's Own Sexuality

Being comfortable about one's own sexuality may be the most important aspect of talking about sex with clients. The therapist needs to be relaxed and open to discussing masturbation, non-normative sexual practices ("kink"), same-sex activities, nonmonogamy, and the whole amazingly wide repertoire of human sexual expression. A therapist need not have personal experience in the sexual activity in order to provide support. The therapist should be open minded and educated in order to understand and appreciate a variety of sexual experiences and acts. One of the best ways therapists can familiarize themselves with a variety of sexual matters is to review the resources in Chapter 11 for appropriate literature and online material. The therapist can gain cultural competency in sexual matters simply by being receptive to others and actively seeking out points of view from a variety of individuals.

Never Assume and Always Assume

Never assume a client's sexual orientation. The use of gender-neutral language early on, such as "partner" instead of "husband" or "boyfriend," will signal an openness to hear a variety of answers. Also, keep the focus on the client's sexual behaviors, not sexual orientation. Men who identify as straight may have occasional, or be the nonreceptive partner in, same-sex encounters. Once a sexual minority feels safe in the interview, he or she will usually declare a sexual orientation, at which point the therapist should use the terms used by the client in referencing sexual partners. Additionally, the therapist should not assume the nature of a client's sexual problem based upon a general demographic profile. For example, it should not be assumed that a woman going through menopause is suffering from a decrease in libido or that a young man's primary problem is premature ejaculation because he says he is not able to last long enough to satisfy his wife.

Conversely, therapists should always assume that everyone does everything, even though people may not talk about it. One couple we treated appeared very conservative and came to treatment because of an affair. Later it was learned that they were both "swingers" and he had gone off with a partner without his wife's knowledge. The earliest sex researcher, Alfred Kinsey, mastered the technique of expecting a wide variety of sexual behaviors in all of his subjects in the phrasing of his questions. By asking, "How frequently do you masturbate?" as opposed to, "Do you masturbate?" the therapist normalizes the behavior, which puts the clients at greater ease. In the event that clients are offended by a question, the therapist should use the situation as an opportunity to join: first by apologizing, next by explaining that he or she deals with a wide variety of sexual matters and wants to make sure to understand their case as fully as possible, and last by seeking information as to what was offensive, such as "I'm sorry to have offended you. Can you tell me—do you have a religious objection to anal intercourse or is it something else?"

Normalize Sex Talk
Sexual history taking can be an opportunity for discovery and relationship building. In sex therapy cases, most clients are ashamed, embarrassed, uncomfortable, or have some difficulty talking openly. The therapist can begin the session with a statement that he or she knows the couple is coming in to improve their sexual life and knows that getting started is difficult for most clients. The therapist can ask the couple how they feel about coming to therapy for help with a sexual problem. The therapist should normalize the feelings, if appropriate, and work to help the couple become more comfortable talking about sexual matters. Normalizing sex talk at the very beginning through a gentle, accepting, matter-of-fact style will

help the clients feel more comfortable and increase their willingness to disclose sensitive information. The therapist may provide an overview of the therapeutic process at this point, allowing the clients to adjust to the situation and surroundings.

Promote Clarity While Using the Client's Language

Because the main objective in taking a sex history is to gain an accurate representation of a client's sexual history and current behavior, it is crucial for the therapist to use the client's language. This use of language will increase the accuracy of the history as well as promote joining. For example, a therapist who asks a client whether he or she suffers from hypoactive sexual desire disorder may not get accurate information because the client lacks knowledge about the meaning of that specific terminology. Like other assessments in psychotherapy, the phrasing of assessment questions should be reflective of a client's educational level, age, and sexual background. In some cases, the therapist would be wise to use the vernacular or slang to inquire about a phenomenon. For example, one highly educated couple (both physicians) used the term "blow job" when referring to oral sex on him. The therapist immediately realized they knew other terminology, but were most comfortable with the term used.

In any case, it is important that the therapist never hesitate to ask for details about the meaning of slang or particular subcultural terms a client may use. For example, even the very general question, "Are you sexually active?" should be clarified. "Sexually active" could mean sexual activity with a partner, but not solitary activities (masturbation) or penile–vaginal penetration, but not oral or anal sex. Clarification of clients' meanings promotes an expectation for description and signals that the therapist is interested in what the clients' experiences have been. The therapist simultaneously provides a role model for the clients in how to ask about unfamiliar or difficult sexual matters and lets them know that their individual experiences are important through encouraging them to convey the personal meaning and import of euphemisms or slang.

Promote the Client's Comfort and Ease in Disclosing

Part of creating comfort for a client can include arranging the room in a certain way, allowing a client to tell his or her story in his or her own way and time, and communicating to the client that he or she is in control of the pace of the assessment and treatment. As stated earlier, the therapist may want to start with some issues that are less threatening and build the client's comfort before moving to more sensitive or threatening issues.

Therapists need to recognize that although they may be used to talking about sexual issues, the client may not be. Therefore, a therapist should invite clients to let the therapist know if he or she is moving too quickly and allow them to control the pace of the assessment.

Therapists should also be aware that to interrupt the process may disrupt the clients' process and concentration and has the potential to elicit denials in behavior. Thus, it is important to let the clients tell their story at their pace. In addition to verbal communication (or silence) indicating client discomfort, the therapist should also attend to body language to infer where a client's comfort level might be. Therapists might notice that a client's body becomes tense or fidgety or that there is a change in the client's tone of voice or pace of speaking with the introduction of a certain topic area. In such cases, the therapist is advised to check routinely with a client and frequently ask how he or she is feeling. Another case we treated involved a highly educated couple referred for sex therapy. As soon as the couple began to talk, the wife covered her entire face with her hand. The therapist stopped the interview to discuss her discomfort. A few minutes later, she was much more comfortable discussing their sexual problem.

Fears about confidentiality may also reduce clients' comfort and level of disclosure. To address this type of discomfort, the therapist should assure each person in treatment of absolute confidentiality. For example, one partner refused to discuss the sexual problems within the office setting because he was concerned that the walls were not soundproofed, although his wife felt comfortable discussing such issues freely. The therapist reassured the couple that no one was able to hear their conversations and further that no one would read their sex history other than the therapist. In order to combat some of the issues related to comfort and disclosure, therapists need to make every effort to be respectful of the clients, understanding their sexual self-schemas and scripts and using their language. In many cases, a little levity will increase clients' comfort, so the therapist should strive to make talking about the issues that have brought clients to treatment an enjoyable exploration rather than a painful exposure.

Interview Individually but Systemically
In some cases, the therapist may experience greater success in treatment if each partner is interviewed independently. Because sexuality can be such a value-laden topic, couples who are interviewed together may not feel comfortable disclosing certain information in front of their partners; they will conceal the information from their partner and, consequently, the therapist. However, it is vital that clients learn to communicate about

sexuality within their relationships. Individual interviews should be conducted only for particularly sensitive areas, rather than for the full clinical history, and typically only if secrets or severe discomfort in disclosing information are suspected. Even when interviewing clients individually, it is important to ask about the systemic impact of the client's problems. The most basic question—"What impact has this problem had on your relationship?"—is usually the most effective. At this point, it is important for the therapist to listen for signs of criticism, defensiveness, contempt, stonewalling, or disengagement, which are strong indicators of a dysfunctional relationship (Gottman, 1994).

Be Clear and Avoid Shaming
Clients may be less willing to disclose information related to their sexual behavior than their emotional relationship, even if sex is the presenting problem in treatment, because of shame or embarrassment. Feelings of shame and embarrassment might prevent clients from asking the therapist to clarify statements and questions. As a result, clients may be responding to items inaccurately and providing some information, but not the complete picture. Such a mismatch in the assessment can have significant implications for the course of treatment. For example, a female client who complains of an inability to achieve orgasm and is uncomfortable discussing masturbation habits or is too embarrassed to ask for clarification when the therapist asks a vague question such as "Do you pleasure yourself?" may leave the therapist with an inaccurate picture of her sexual functioning. The therapist may diagnose the client with primary, lifelong anorgasmia because of miscommunication.

The couple or family system may be set up in a way that prevents the clients from believing that it is permissible to discuss the details of their sexual life. It is possible to have clients acknowledge there is a sexual concern and seek treatment, but internally be struggling with messages censoring their disclosure from either their family of origin or their partner, based on the rules around sexual disclosure within that system. In a case where a couple sought treatment for the husband's erectile dysfunction, the therapist asked about previous discord related to sexuality within the couple's relationship. As the wife began to answer, the husband interrupted his wife and told her not to talk about it because he believed the therapist did not need to know that particular information about them. The therapist did not work to decrease the couple's sense of shame; rather, she tried to convince the couple that the information was important. The more the therapist tried to convince, the more adamant the husband was that the information was within the couple and not to be shared. The wife became silent on that topic, thus respecting the rules of the relationship but ultimately complicating the treatment process. Frequently, the rules of what can and cannot be shared are unspoken, and the therapist has little knowledge of what is not being disclosed unless a concerted effort is made to make the clients feel comfortable disclosing sensitive sexual and relationship information.

Assessment questions should avoid indicating a socially desirable answer. Compare the question "Have you been unfaithful?" to "Do you have sexual relations with others in addition to your primary partner?" The former has been phrased in a way that may not be clear to the clients (what is meant by "faithful"?) and promotes a socially preferred answer because few people believe being unfaithful is acceptable. The second question gets information that is far more accurate and does not imply a certain way to answer, thereby normalizing the client's sexual experiences. Similarly, the therapist should not suggest answers. When a client reports that his erections last "less than normal," the therapist should be sure not to suggest an answer by saying "so, about 3½ minutes?" In such a case, the therapist might be signaling that erections should last a particular length of time, when the reality is that "normal" sexual behavior varies from person to person and with an individual over time.

Throughout the interview process, the therapist should adopt an attitude that conveys matter-of-fact neutrality, professionalism, and genuinely warm support. As the client discloses information, the therapist needs to be aware of body language and responses, being cautious to refrain from behaving in a way that would appear judgmental. This includes avoiding reactions that communicate surprise or disapproval by monitoring voice inflection, facial expressions, and other behaviors.

Lastly, the client may have a disability, illness, or other medical/health issue that complicates the sexual problem. For example, diabetes can contribute to erectile dysfunction. In such cases, the medical problem affects physical aspects of one's sexual desire and performance, the roles in the sexual relationship, and thoughts and feelings about sex (Valentich & Gripton, 1984; Weeks & Gambescia, 2000). The therapist should be knowledgeable about the client's physical history and any contributing illnesses and be sure that the history that was taken accounts for the wide variety of etiology of the problem.

Conducting an Intersystems Clinical Interview

Applying an Intersystems approach, the sexual history would address four levels:

1. the individual level, assessing each partner's physical and mental well-being;
2. the interpersonal level, inquiring into the relationship dynamics and history;
3. family of origin, asking about overt and covert messages in the family, openness to sexuality, etc.; and
4. the sociocultural level, assessing contextual factors as they impact both the individual and interpersonal levels—for example, how religious beliefs might influence sexual behavior.

Conducting the Clinical Interview

First, the therapist needs to review any intake forms or other written assessment information before meeting with the clients. Next, each partner is allowed to talk about the problem, as the therapist uses the first few of the following questions. The therapist should be sure to get the most essential information before asking questions that are specific to the particular sexual dysfunction. Essential questions include:

- What are the reasons you are coming in? What seems to be the problem?
- Why are you seeking treatment at this time?
- What treatments or things have you tried already to fix this problem on your own? What was the result? Did some things work better than others did?
- What are your goals for this therapy? How would you like your sexual experiences to be?
- What is your or your partner's theory for this problem?
- To what extent does this problem distress you and your partner?
- What impact has it had on you? On your partner? On your relationship?

From there, the therapist begins to delve more deeply into the factors surrounding the main sexual problems as identified by the clients or to elaborate on pertinent issues on each of the three systems levels. Typically, it is easier to review and expand on the biological, move to the sociocultural, and then address the psychological, interpersonal, and family of origin.

Individual Factors—Biological

The clinical interview should include a review of general health and specific medical conditions—particularly hormonal, cardiovascular, or neurological disorders that might impact sexual functioning listed on any intake forms. Adopting a nonjudgmental approach, the therapist should ask about lifestyle factors, including diet, tobacco, alcohol and recreational drug use, level of exercise, and stress levels, which can impact the etiology of a sexual dysfunction as well as the course of treatment. Appropriate psychoeducational material can be presented to the client in the questioning, such as:

> I'd like to know about your smoking habits because the nicotine in cigarettes is a vasoconstrictor, which means it closes down the blood vessels, making it difficult for some men to have an erection. I would like to suggest the following book or Internet site to you.

The therapist should also inquire about prescription medication use, particularly selective serotonin reuptake inhibitor (SSRI) antidepressants (such as Prozac), antihypertensives (beta-blockers and calcium channel antagonists), and antipsychotics or other psychotropic medicines. The chapter by Verhulst and Reynolds in *Systemic Sex Therapy* (Hertlein, Weeks, & Gambescia, 2008) provides a comprehensive overview of the sexual side effects of a wide variety of recreational and prescription drugs.

Individual Factors—Psychological

The interview should establish the client's current levels of stress and coping mechanisms, general affect and cognitive functioning, history of mental disturbances, and previous emotional, mental, or sexual trauma. The therapist will want to know about the clients' perceptions of self and others, especially significant others, lovers, parents, and authority figures. Psychosexual issues, including the ability to fantasize, sexual self-schemas, and conceptions about sex internalized from early experiences and family-of-origin messages, should also be addressed. Of utmost importance is to determine the level of distress the clients are experiencing from the sexual problem and how they manage that distress. Clients can vary greatly concerning how personally distressed they are about a problem. The therapist should always look for a discrepancy in level of distress between partners. Sometimes the clients' responses will indicate the need to assess further for substance abuse or mood and/or anxiety disorders—particularly depression—because these disorders are so common and linked to sexual problems.

Relational Factors

It is rare that clients present sexual dysfunctions for treatment without partner relational problems of a sexual nature or significant impacts on the other partner. Thus, assessing for comorbidity of partner sexual problems and relationship risk factors is crucial to developing an effective treatment plan. Some basic questions involve sexual communication within the couple as well as the technical skills and sexual repertoire of each partner. More relationally oriented questions to begin with would include current relationship dynamics, including unresolved anger or recurrent conflict, communication styles, and projections and defenses. Next, the therapist will want to ask about levels of and expectations for intimacy; discrepancies in sexual styles or drives; levels of physical, sexual, and other attraction to the partner; and the ability to get sexual and intimacy needs met within the relationship. This can be the most difficult part of the clinical interview, and it may best be done with a "mine, yours, and ours" format, with individual interviews over one or two sessions, followed by one or more conjoint sessions.

Sociocontextual Factors

Although it is the outermost level, assessing the sociocultural level and contextual factors as they impact both the individual and interpersonal levels may best be done earlier in the clinical interview. The questions are typically less threatening, and knowing the clients' sexual mores and cultural norms will aid the therapist in structuring the rest of the interview, as well as knowing the appropriate language to use in formulating specific questions.

The therapist should begin by asking about gender roles in the initiation of sexual activity, gendered expectations regarding sexuality, and beliefs about the role and function of sex, pleasure, procreation, and contraception. The therapist should be sure to look for particular ethnocultural or religious mandates about sexual propriety and adherence to societal sexual scripts. Questions that are more sensitive would include beliefs about and the practice of non-normative sexual practices or "kink," which may be addressed at the same time as other individual psychosexual matters. When assessing the broader sociocultural impact, it is wise to honor the individuality of the client, maintaining the "not-knowing" stance that prevents premature identification of the problem, as well as stereotyping and labeling of the client.

Family of Origin
Questions about the family of origin are sometimes best asked later during the assessment process. Couples with sexual problems often do not see any connection between their early life experiences and what they are experiencing today. Thus, they may think the therapist is incompetent or bring up old painful issues for no reason. The therapist may begin with a basic genogram and focus on questions relating to attachment, intimacy, and sexuality within the family. The overall family environment strongly influences one's emotional development, which is then focused sexually. Specific sexual messages (covert and overt) may need to be explored carefully.

Interviewing for Specific Disorders

Clinicians assess a variety of elements during a sexual history. The basic task is to render a differential diagnosis or one where certain problems are ruled in and others are ruled out. One aspect of the sex history is trying to uncover the presence of a *DSM-IV-TR* disorder, be it a sexual dysfunction or a comorbid disorder that impacts sexual functioning or satisfaction. In such cases, it is important to include questions around differential diagnoses and inquire as to whether the symptoms have a biological or organic basis or are psychogenic and possibly secondary to another psychological disorder. Chapter 3 provides details on the features of each disorder; however, specific questions to make a diagnosis and begin the process of developing a case formulation follow for each dysfunction. In asking these questions, it is important to keep them in the context of an Intersystems sexual history because, for example, knowing about sexual satisfaction independently of the overall couple relationship will provide an incomplete picture, leading to inaccurate case formulation and ineffective treatment plans.

Sexual Desire Disorders

Hypoactive Sexual Desire Disorder
The presence of negative sexual thoughts and no sexual thoughts can contribute to a lack of desire. Hypoactive sexual desire disorder (HSDD) is

one of the most complex of all sexual problems. A number of psychological factors are usually working together to suppress sexual desire, making the assessment of this problem time consuming, complex, and involving many questions over the course of several sessions. Weeks and Gambescia (2002) proposed that positive sexual thoughts and/or fantasies are essential for desire. Therefore, assessing for the presence of negative sexual thoughts or a lack of sexual fantasies is important in determining HSDD. A key part to the assessment of sexual desire is to ask the clients about the five domains described in Table 2.2.

A key part of our rapid assessment of lack of sexual desire is to ask the client to list the negative sexual thoughts or cognitions in four categories. These categories are listed in Table 2.3. The therapist inquires about aspects of each partner's desire, including: (1) frequency of sex, (2) frequency of sexual desire, (3) degree of sexual interest, (4) context of sexual desire, and (5) presence of other sexual dysfunctions of difficulties. Some typical questions to ask in order to assess these areas include:

- How often do you actually have sex in a week, month, or year (on average)?
- How often do you feel like having sex?
- Do you believe your level of desire is too low, too high?
- When did you first notice that you were losing your sexual desire?
- What was happening at the time that might account for the loss of desire?
- Did you lose your desire suddenly or gradually?
- What was your level of desire early in the relationship, over the course of the relationship, now?
- What medications are you taking now or since losing your desire?
- Have there been any changes in your health?
- On a scale from −10 to 10, with 0 being neutral desire, where would you place your desire (most of the time, prior to sex, during sex, after sex, when you know your partner wants sex, etc.)?
- If you feel desire and it is suddenly lost, what are the circumstances? What are you thinking at the moment it is lost?
- Do you feel a lack of desire for your partner or for everyone?
- To what extent does your desire distress you and your partner?
- What are your theory and your partner's theory for your lack of desire?

Sexual Aversion Disorder
Sexual aversion disorder (SAD) frequently has a similar etiology to that of HSDD and is more commonly seen in women than in men. The distress experienced is typically interpersonal, in that a client will present for treatment only after being told by a partner that there is something

TABLE 2.2 Domains of Desire Assessment

Domain	Assessment items
Frequency of sex	How often do you engage in affectionate or sexual behaviors (cuddling, kissing, holding hands, back rubs, etc.) in a week, month, or year?
	How often do you actually have sex in a week, month, or year?
Frequency of sexual desire	How often do you feel like having sex?
	Do you feel the frequency of your wanting to have sex is a problem?
Context of sexual desire	Do you ever feel "sexy" or sexually desirable? How often? When? With whom?
	Do you ever feel desire for your partner? For someone else you know? For people you do not know personally, like movie stars or fictional characters?
	Do you feel desire for sex without it being attached to anything or any person?
	What was your level of desire early in the relationship, over the course of the relationship, now?
	When did you first notice that your sexual desire had changed?
Degree of sexual arousal and satisfaction	Are you happy with how often you have sex?
	Do you usually enjoy having sex? Do you achieve orgasm?
	Do you feel as though you can become easily aroused (for women this would include lubrication; for men, the ability to obtain and maintain an erection)?
	How much time do you devote to sexual activity, including "foreplay"?
	What do you find most pleasurable?
Presence of other sexual dysfunctions or difficulties	Do you wish your lovemaking could be different? How so?
	Does your partner seem to enjoy sex?
	Do you have concerns or worries about you or your partner regarding sex?

"wrong" with him or her. In interviewing suspected cases of SAD, it is of utmost importance to work at the pace set by the client and build trust because there may be a history of emotional or sexual abuse. We recommend using a scale such as the one in Figure 2.1, ranging from –10 to 10,

TABLE 2.3 Rapid Assessment Items

Area	Sample cognitions
Self	I don't like sex
	I hate the way my body looks
	I don't know what my partner really wants
Partner	My partner is selfish sexually
	My partner is too rough
	My partner never wants to give me any foreplay or romance
Relationship	We always fight about sex
	We have never had good sex
	We never seem to be on the same page sexually
Other	My family taught me that sex was an obligation
	My family never really talked about sex
	My church is very negative about sex

to assess both motivations for sexual encounters and feelings of arousal in sexual experiences.

Depending upon the information obtained previously, the therapist would ask the client the following questions:

- Where would you generally place yourself and your partner on this scale?
- Where would you place yourself and your partner just prior to initiation of sex?
- Where would you place yourself and your partner when your partner initiates any sexual activity?
- Where would you place yourself and your partner when you think about or imagine having sex?
- Where would you place yourself and your partner during sexual activity?
- Where would you place yourself and your partner when your relationship is going well?
- Where would you place yourself and your partner when your relationship is not working?
- How distressed do you feel when a sexual interaction is being initiated? How much anxiety or panic do you feel, if any?
- Where would you place yourself on this scale prior to, during, and after solo sex or masturbation?

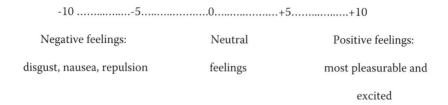

-10 ....-5.....................0.....................+5................+10

Negative feelings:	Neutral	Positive feelings:
disgust, nausea, repulsion	feelings	most pleasurable and
		excited

Figure 2.1   Motivation assessment scale.

Hyperactive Sexual Desire/Sexual Compulsivity

Sexual addiction is often difficult to diagnose because it may be masked by other psychiatric disorders, such as anxiety, depression, bipolar illness, hypomania, obsessive–compulsive personality disorder, and so on. Further, it may be present along with other forms of addiction, post-traumatic stress disorder, or childhood sexual abuse (Turner, 2008). Based on the work of Carnes (1987; 1990), the following questions can be used when beginning to assess for sexual addiction:

- How would you describe your feelings prior to, during, and after having a sexual encounter? Do your moods change dramatically surrounding sexual activity?
- Have bad things happened because of your sexual behavior?
- Do you wish that you could limit your sexual behavior?
- Do you try unsuccessfully to manage your sexual behavior?
- Do you enjoy doing risky things like speeding, doing drugs, or stealing? Do you practice safe sex in every sexual encounter?
- When you are stressed or worried, do you find yourself thinking about sex or rehearsing a sexual fantasy in your mind?
- Have you increased the number or degree of risk of your sexual acts over time?
- How much time would you say you spend thinking about or pursuing sexual encounters?
- Have you neglected important social, occupational, or recreational activities because you were thinking about or pursuing sex?

We recommend that a picture of the sexual acting out be gained before asking these questions—for example, whether the acting out is with pornography, other men or women, or prostitutes; behaviors that are not mainstream sex, such as sadism and masochism, etc.

Sexual Arousal Disorders

Male Erectile Dysfunction

In assessing for erectile dysfunction (ED), it is important to have the results of a recent physical examination by a physician or urologist who is well trained in the etiology of sexual dysfunction. It is now known that, as men grow older, the chances of medical problems and medication use, especially blood pressure medications, can cause greater interference with erectile ability. Thus, establishing the etiology—physiological, psychogenic, or a combination of the erectile difficulties—is paramount. The following questions help the therapist begin to understand some of the fundamental causes. A thorough description of causes and assessment has been described in Weeks and Gambescia (2000). Beginning questions would include:

- Have you seen a doctor or urologist for this problem?
- When did you last have a physical and were there any problems?
- Do you have any problems with your heart or circulation? Do you have any diabetes or neurological problems? Has there been any trauma to your pelvis (including extensive bike riding)?
- Are you taking any medications?
- When did you first notice a problem with your erections?
- Did your problem begin suddenly or gradually?
- When you attempt sexual activity, at what point do you begin to lose the erection? Can you get it back if you lose it?
- Do certain positions work better than others in keeping the erection?

Once etiology has been determined, the following questions will assist in assessing the level of performance anxiety and any related dysfunctions:

- Do you try to will yourself to have a strong erection? What happens when you do this?
- What thoughts do you now have about being able to keep an erection? Do you feel anxious about losing it?
- How do you and your partner react to losing your erection?
- Has this problem led to avoiding sex with your partner?

Female Sexual Arousal Disorder

Like ED, female sexual arousal disorder (FSAD) is highly related to age, frequently occurring in menopausal and postmenopausal women and arising from both physiological as well as psychological conditions. It can be comorbid with both HSDD and inorgasmia, as well as a range of diagnosable conditions, particularly depression (Lewis et al., 2004). As such, it is important to assess for hormonal, cardiovascular, neurological, and psychiatric conditions. Also important is a detailed understanding of why the woman is currently seeking treatment; often, her level of distress over the problem may be less than her partner's level of distress, complicating her motivation to undergo treatment. In addition to the questions listed for HSDD, the following get at the client's subjective understanding of her desire:

- Do you feel aroused by sexual thoughts, fantasies, reading a sexy passage in a book, or seeing a sexy scene in a movie?
- Do you feel aroused by having different parts of your body touched (by yourself or your partner)?
- What parts of your body do you most like having touched?
- What kinds of stimulation (hand–genital, mouth–genital, genital–genital, sex toy–genital) are most pleasurable?
- Do you feel comfortable talking with your partner about what you like?
- Do you lubricate enough to make sex comfortable? Have you tried using lubricants; if so, which ones? Do you think they are effective?

Orgasmic Disorders

Premature Ejaculation

Premature ejaculation (PE) is the most common sexual problem found in men, with studies indicating that one third of men in the United States having experienced recurrent premature ejaculation (Laumann, Paik, & Rosen, 1999). Although retrograde ejaculation and emission phase disorders are likely due to physiological abnormalities, biogenic PE typically arises in conjunction with lifestyle risks (such as cigarette smoking and stress) or because of other health problems, notably arteriosclerosis and diabetes. Because psychogenic PE involves the inability to control when ejaculation occurs, assessment should focus more on the subjective experience of controlling one's ejaculation rather than the actual length of time between penetration and ejaculation. Some assessment questions include:

- Do you think you ejaculate too quickly? Does your partner share your belief?
- Have there been times when your control is better; if so, under what conditions?
- When did your ability to delay ejaculation first become a problem?

- Have you had any significant health changes?
- Do you believe that the force and volume of your ejaculate are appropriate?
- Do you ever have pain or discomfort upon ejaculation?
- How do you and your partner react when you ejaculate too quickly?
- Have you ever become panicked at the thought of ejaculating too quickly? Are there other times when you feel panicky?
- How much pressure do you put on yourself not to ejaculate?
- Are you or your partner less satisfied with sexual experiences that culminate too quickly?
- Do thoughts that you will not last long enough keep you from engaging in sexual activity?
- Does your partner's belief that you will not last long enough stop your partner from engaging in sexual activity?

Female Orgasmic Disorder

In female orgasmic disorder, the client is unable to reach orgasm with what is typically seen as sufficient stimulation.* Some women may report that they have never had an orgasm or are unsure if they have ever experienced orgasm. Others will report a decrease of pleasure or sensation or increased difficulty in reaching orgasm. Some cases of female orgasmic disorder (FOD) may have an organic basis, such as diabetes, spinal cord injuries, or use of medication such as SSRIs. However, most cases involve some combination of inexperience and psychological and psychosocial factors. Mah and Binik (2002) advocate assessing the cognitive–affective and sensory elements of sexual pleasure, rather than just the physiological responses women may believe are necessary for orgasm. Assessment questions that provide a more detailed and subjective picture of the woman's sexuality include:

- Are you taking any medications or do you have any physical problems? Do you know if your hormonal levels are normal?
- Do you typically enjoy sensual/sexual experiences?
- Have you ever in your life experienced an orgasm? In the past, could you have orgasms more easily or at all? How has your orgasmic ability changed over time?
- If you have never had an orgasm, what do you imagine will happen when you do? What do you imagine it will feel like?

---

* Inorgasmia is an older term and the one that most clients adopt. Therefore, we will use the term "inorgasmia" for the rest of this text.

- What forms of stimulation (vibrator, manual [with hand], oral, intercourse), if any, do you use to become aroused? With what forms of stimulation do you most easily achieve orgasm? What is the most difficult way to achieve orgasm?
- How difficult is it for you to achieve orgasm through manual stimulation (vibrator, with hand, oral) and during intercourse?
- How much stimulation do you typically need to become stimulated or to reach orgasm? What do you feel with this form of stimulation? What are your subjective sensations?
- Do you feel sexually satisfied if you do not have an orgasm?
- Do you feel you are disappointing your partner if you do not have an orgasm?
- Do you feel that you sometimes get close to orgasm but cannot quite get there?
- Has the level of sexual pleasure you experience changed over time?
- How has your ability to be sexually aroused, orgasmic, and sexually satisfied changed?
- When you have intercourse, about how long does it last? Do you feel you must have an orgasm for yourself? for your partner?
- What happens when you try to have an orgasm now?
- If you can achieve orgasm, what percent of the time can you do so if that is what you want?
- Do you pressure yourself to reach an orgasm? Does your partner pressure you to have an orgasm?
- Do you feel your orgasm is yours or is it for the sake of your partner?
- What is your goal for this therapy? How would you like to be able to achieve orgasm if that is your goal?
- Do you masturbate? At what age did you begin to stimulate yourself? Did you have an orgasm? Do you feel your orgasm is yours or is it for the sake of your partner?
- If you have never had an orgasm, what do you imagine will happen when you do? What do you imagine it will feel like?
- Do you believe there is any reason why women should or should not masturbate and should or should not reach orgasm or enjoy sex? Is there anything negative associated with having an orgasm (such as losing control, getting addicted to it, your partner having some power over you, losing your mind, etc.)?
- What is your theory about why you do not have orgasms?

Sexual Pain Disorders

Vaginusmus and Dysparenuia

These disorders are ones in which the woman experiences pain or discomfort with orgasm. There appears to be great confusion in the medical literature, with the two terms used interchangeably. Vaginusmus is generally considered to be psychogenic, while dysparenuia is organic. The reader should consult Hertlein et al. (2008) and Leiblum (2007; 2008) for current information on this topic. Women with vaginusmus often have difficulty with penetration because the muscle surrounding the vaginal opening tightens up or goes into spasm. Because there is typically a mixed etiology, assessment must focus on both physical and psychological factors. Appropriate questions include:

- Describe what happens when you attempt any type of penetration. What do you feel with digital penetration (a finger), tampon, a penis, or other object?
- What exactly do you feel? Is it a burning, stretching, tearing, or other type of sensation? Where do you feel the sensation?
- Have you seen a gynecologist for this problem? What did he or she find? Have you had vaginal infections, an accident causing pain, or any other kind of pain in the genital region?
- How long have you had this problem? Has it changed over time?
- Have you ever experienced any kind of sexual trauma, especially rape or incest?
- Can you sometimes have intercourse without pain or other types of penetration without pain or discomfort?
- To what extent are you afraid your partner will hurt you during sex?
- On a scale from 1 to 10, how fearful are you before some type of penetration (specify types)?
- Are you able to calm down and relax after penetration?
- Are you usually lubricated prior to penetration? Have you used lubricants? What types?
- Do you find that you avoid all types of sexual interactions because of the fear of pain?
- Can you think of any negative consequence of having intercourse (e.g., fear of pregnancy, getting diseases, losing control, religious reason, etc.) What impact has this problem had on your relationship?
- Why are you coming to treatment at this particular time?

Most gynecologists are not well trained in making a differential diagnosis and the therapist can only guess what might be the actual problem.

The therapist will need to find a well-trained obstetrician–gynecologist. A few gynecologists in the United States are board certified in gynecology and infectious disease. These doctors can find problems that most other gynecologists never consider and they know how to treat them.

Remember that all the disorders described previously are much more complex than the questions reflect. The therapist can use these questions as beginnings, probing further with additional questions that derive from the replies in order to obtain as complete a picture of the presenting problem as possible. The client's answers to the preceding questions are best seen as a point of departure for additional questions.

Focused Genograms

A focused genogram is a type of focused assessment that allows therapists to obtain relational, dynamic, and intergenerational information about the sexual aspects of the clients and their relationship. This section reviews the importance and application of focused genograms, gives an overview of techniques for administration, and provides questions for three different types of focused genograms: gender, romantic love, and sexuality. The therapist should review all of the questions in each of the three genograms and select those that are most appropriate, tailoring the genogram design to each particular case.

Importance and Application

Sexuality is deeply connected to sex-role learning and cognitive-belief systems that arise through family-of-origin interactions as well as cultural and religious processes of socialization (Kimmel, 2007; Money, 1986). Although both men and women experience sexual desire and arousal, they may think and feel differently about sex, based in part on the messages they took from their families, their larger sociocultural milieu, and the media's messages throughout life. Beyond sexuality, an understanding of the role that romantic love plays may be of importance. Romance involves physiologic arousal, sexual longing, intense focus on the loved one, and a particular kind of idealization. The question of how one knew that one was loved in the family and what one was loved for may be central to a greater understanding of the complexity of the couple relationship.

The therapist may want to complete a focused genogram when intergenerational dynamics or constrictive sexual scripts are suspected of bringing on or maintaining a sexual problem or there is evidence of relational comorbidity. In order for the genogram to be useful in treating sexual dysfunctions, it is important to move beyond merely chronicling family events to depicting visually the clients' perceptions of relationship patterns and responses to crisis, change, or developmental transitions (McGoldrick & Gerson, 1985; McGoldrick, Gerson, & Shellenberger, 1999; Thomas, 1998). In keeping with the Intersystems perspective, the genograms presented here readily obtain information on the personal, interpersonal, and sociocultural levels, at once explicating relational patterns as well as possible sources of dysfunctional or constrictive messages surrounding sexuality.

Administering a Genogram

Hof and Berman (1986) see the development of sexual genograms as a five-stage process:

- introduction;
- creation and exploration of a general genogram;
- creation and exploration of the sexual genogram;
- discussion of genogram material with the couple; and
- total review of the process with incorporation into the treatment plan.

Some of the information in a general genogram may be redundant with intake or sexual history data, so each of these five steps may not be necessary. It is important, however, that the therapist fully inform the client of the process and obtain the client's full participation because the sexual themes uncovered in the genogram may be a serious and an important part of the problem the client is experiencing.

In addition to assessment, a well-crafted genogram can serve as an opportunity for positive attitudinal, emotional, or behavioral change. The concept of focused genograms and a wide range of focused genograms represented a great leap forward in assessment using genograms (DeMaria, Weeks, & Hof, 1999). As noted, adequately preparing a client involves, at a minimum:

- the therapist and client working in collaboration in the creation and application of a genogram;

- full explanation of the particular genogram that the therapist has in mind, along with a rationale for the process and what is to be learned; and
- ensuring that the client appreciates the value of the focused genogram and is willing to go through the process of discovery because even though self-assessment genograms are relatively easy to do, there is a degree of anxiety attached to sexual issues.

Focused genograms are best administered only after clients and therapist have established a therapeutic relationship and trust has developed. It is often useful to start by asking the client to take the genogram questions home and answer them in private in preparation for sharing with a partner or the therapist. In cases where one partner is the "identified patient," it is important to get the partner's sense of the family's sexual issues, which can be best done in a conjoint session devoted to an initial review of the client's answers.

Because historical time and culture affect sexual patterns, it is helpful to know specifically the parents' ages, the decade of the client's childhood, and whether the child or parents were immigrants. When information is required from the clients' parents, it is important to counsel caution, advising that clients start with questions about beliefs and education. It is also not necessary or advisable for the client to get the details of parents' sex lives or share his or her own sex life with parents. (If an adult child has a specific dysfunction, it is sometimes helpful to know if a parent had the same problem and how he or she solved it.) Although therapists are encouraged to tailor questions to the unique aspects of their cases, we present the gender, sexuality, and romantic love genograms separately because each area has its own definitions, issues, and ordering.

Gender Genograms

Gender genograms examine the fit of beliefs and practice about gender among the culture, family, and person by focusing on general beliefs about men and women, family patterns of closeness and dominance, issues around work and money, sexuality, reproductive events, sexual orientation, and physical and psychological dysfunction. Many of the most common relational problems in clinical practice, to some extent, have origins in gender socialization and self-schemas. Questions for the gender genogram can be found in Table 2.4.

TABLE 2.4   Gender Genogram Questions

Intersystems dimension	Specific domain	Assessment items
Dyadic	Family beliefs about being a man or a woman	What does the family believe about what men and women should do in the world? Does this change over the life cycle?
		What are family beliefs about marriage and the roles of men and women in marriage?
		What defines masculinity and femininity? What do you have to do or be to become an adult man or woman in the family?
		What are the family beliefs about money? Who earns it, who controls it, who spends it, who saves it? How gender specific are these patterns?
		Are the messages given by men and women in the family contradictory or consistent? If mixed messages are given, who says what? How gender stereotyped are the messages?
		Is one gender considered superior to the other? On what basis?
Family of origin	Gender and work	What is the educational level and occupation of all members of the family of origin? Are there gender-specific patterns of jobs or career choices?
		For those with careers, were they successful? How is success or failure at work defined in the family? Are the men or the women in the family, as a group, considered more successful at work?
		Is child care or volunteer work valued or considered a career?
		If there is inherited wealth in the family, are men or women more likely to inherit or to be given control over the money?
	Family patterns of relationships	What are the patterns of relationships in terms of closeness or distance; showing emotions; taking, giving, or sharing power?
		Do men and women show their needs for closeness and distance differently?
		Do relationships generally tend toward an egalitarian model?

	Couple relationship patterns	What are the patterns of affairs, divorces, abandonment, loyalty, and sacrifice by men and women in the family? Family honor and shame Who are the family heroes and heroines? For what are they honored? Are there more men or women honored? Are the family villains male or female? What are their crimes?
	Family impact on current gender behavior	How close do you come to fulfilling your family's expectations for your sex? How have you gone about trying to conform to or rebel against these expectations? What positive or negative effects have these expectations had on your life? How have you struggled to overcome the negative effects? If you are married or in a serious relationship, how close do you and your partner come to meeting expectations of marriages, of being a husband or wife? How have family expectations regarding gender affected your relationship? Under what circumstances do you have the most positive image of yourself in your relationship? The most negative? In what ways does your partner live up to your ideal wife, husband, or partner?
Sociocultural	Peer expectations	How have the standards of your peer group concerning male and female roles affected your life? Have there been different peer groups with different standards over the years to whom you have related? When these groups are in conflict, which set of standards is most compelling to you? How have you dealt with the pressure to conform to these standards? Which standards do you consider desirable or undesirable? How is your self-image affected if you fail to attain these standards?
	Cultural expectations	Who were your idols growing up (real or fictional)? What did they model as desirable male or female qualities? Which did you try to emulate and how did this affect your life? What effect did these models have on your expectations of relationships? What impact are they having on your current relationships? What is the effect of mass media (television, films, books, etc.) on your ideas about male and female roles and your current relationship?

Sexual Genograms

Sexual genograms investigate the sexual development that took place within the family and how family members, teachers, peers, and others influenced sexual beliefs and practices (Berman & Hof, 1987). The sexual genogram is most helpful in defining and deconstructing the family attitudes and beliefs about sexuality that result in the development of specific love maps or scripts in the client. In asking these questions, therapists should focus first on general beliefs about men and women and family patterns of closeness and dominance, moving on to reproductive events, sexual orientation issues, and the development and sharing of sexual knowledge over one or more sessions.

Hof and Berman (1986) report that the sexual genogram is most effective if conducted after an initial evaluation. The five main parts of this genogram include: (1) introduction, (2) creation and exploration of a standard genogram, (3) creation and exploration of a sexual genogram, (4) exploration and discussion of genogram with family members, and (5) integration of the genogram into treatment. The therapist explains the utility of a genogram in its relation to client functioning and may provide an example. The therapist can then work with the clients to help them focus their genogram on the sexual concerns. The therapist also educates the couple on how to construct a standard genogram, including a discussion of the appropriate symbols to use, etc. Once the standard genogram is completed, the therapist guides the clients into focusing the genogram on the sexual concern by inquiring about the messages conveyed to the clients from their families of origin related to sexuality, questions assessing how sexuality was discussed in the home and between generations, an assessment of secrets around sexuality, how discussions could have been handled regarding sexuality, and what their partners think of their genograms. During the exploration and discussion phase, Hof and Berman remind readers that sharing of the content within a genogram can raise anxiety and fear and that this is critically important when developing a sexual genogram. Finally, the therapist consolidates the exercise for the couple by asking what they learned from doing the genogram and what application it can have for their sexual problems.

Questions for the sexual genogram include:

- What were the overt and covert messages in your family regarding sexuality, intimacy, masculinity, femininity?

- Was anyone constrained or inhibited in communicating about sexuality, affection, intimacy, and other feelings that showed warmth?
- Who said or did what? Who was conspicuously silent or absent in the area of sexuality and intimacy?
- Who expressed the most intimacy and in what ways?
- Who expressed the least intimacy? What was the effect?
- Who was the most open sexually and in what ways?
- Who was the least open sexually and in what ways?
- How were intimacy, affection, and sexuality encouraged or discouraged?
- What questions did you want to ask about sexuality but were afraid to do so?
- Do you know of any "secrets" in your family regarding sexuality and intimacy (e.g., incest, unwanted pregnancies, or extramarital affairs)? What were they? How were they handled by various family members?
- How do you think other members of your family would answer these questions?
- How does your current partner view your sexual upbringing, history, and family values and beliefs? How do you perceive your partner's sexual upbringing?
- What would you have like to have changed about the way your family discussed and showed their intimacy, affection, and sexuality?
- Were any members of your family treated as outcasts because of their sexuality? To what effect?
- How do you see your sexuality today connected to what you learned in your family?

DeMaria et al. (1999) further developed the sexual genogram in a book on focused genograms. They realized that sexuality could not be separated from many other facts of the system and thus recommended the use of the gender, sexuality, and love genograms as a group in better assessing the sexual problem. They also developed dozens of other types of topically oriented genograms—focused genograms. Attachment genograms are also useful additions to the other genograms mentioned. Each focused genogram is a series of systematically organized questions. These questions are embedded within a theoretical framework and include treatment suggestions.

Romantic Love Genograms

Uncovering patterns of unrequited love, loss, or abandonment may be important in treating sexual dysfunctions because the ways in which many people actually embrace and re-create or feel compelled to resist their parents' patterns in these areas can impact their sexual functioning within romantic relationships. Love relationships in the family of origin provide a powerful template for future behavior, especially in the area of ongoing intimacy. Questions about romantic intimacy include:

- How were intimacy and love displayed in your family by men and women?
- How did your parents show love toward each other? Toward the children? How were children expected to show love? What did you have to do to receive love (perform academically, be beautiful, be a loving family member)?
- Did loving involve primarily caretaking, listening, and/or saying loving things?
- Who were the most and the least loving in your extended family? Who were the most and the least loved in your family?
- Who in the family was abandoned or abandoned others?
- Were loved ones lost through death or tragedy?

Items assessing romantic love include:

- How was romantic love shown in your family?
- What is the story of your parents' courtship? Are there other well-known stories of courtship in the family?
- Are there family patterns of divorce or abandonment during courtship or after marriage?
- Did the family believe in "love at first sight," or did "true love" develop slowly? Was being in love a good reason or the only reason to get married, or were other reasons more powerful?
- In order to be in love, were you supposed to be passionate, jealous, demanding, or more of a good friend?
- Was love seen as logical or beyond logic?
- If you were in love with a person of the wrong cultural background or your parents did not approve, were you expected to give up the lover or the parents?
- If you fell in love, could you still be loyal to friends, other family members, and so forth?
- Was falling in love considered an acceptable reason to have an affair?
- If you loved someone who did not love you back, was this cause for despair?

The gender, sexuality, and romantic love genograms presented here provide a mechanism for understanding clients' intergenerational influences on their everyday experiences of being men and women, their sexuality, and their beliefs and fears about love and intimacy. Because men and women may present with sexual concerns that are frequently linked to gender, sexual genograms together with gender genograms may be important in delving into family norms and values that affect sexual scripts, styles, and beliefs. The function and meaning of sexual behaviors are deeply embedded in gender conditioning and therefore questions should be asked specifically about the intersection of sex and gender (e.g., "What is your image of what a real man and a real woman are like in bed?").

In addition to constructing genograms, therapists could use these questions to develop either a family love map or a sexual knowledge/trauma time line. Family maps reveal patterns of gender identification, love, and conflict, which provide a template for further experiences by focusing on patterns of closeness and distance with parents and significant others. As the ability to fuse lust and tenderness, love and commitment, and kindness and assertiveness is learned in the family, evidence of rigid gender or sex rules in a family map may indicate ways in which the client is poorly suited to the basic complexity of adult sexual love. A sexual time line would contain elements of significance as the client moves developmentally from childhood to adult love relationships, including incidents of sexual awakening or trauma in childhood and adult life. Such a time line is most helpful in focusing on clients' increasing conscious knowledge of their own sexual responses as well as their parents' responses to their developing sexuality, which may be projected onto current partners in adult life.

3

Step-by-Step Diagnosis of Sexual Dysfunctions

> Diagnosis is more than identifying a disorder (nosological diagnosis) or distinguishing one disorder from another (differential diagnosis); diagnosis is the thorough understanding of what is going on in the mind and the body of the person who presents for care.
>
> Mezzich and Hernandez-Serrano (2006, p. 47)

Introduction

Diagnosis of sexual dysfunctions may seem straightforward in that clients may describe difficulties that are clearly matters of desire or clearly an issue of orgasm. However, diagnosis is never quite as straightforward as it appears. Even in cases like erectile dysfunction, understanding how the problem occurred (etiology) is just as important as discerning what is happening (the differential diagnosis). A multiaxial diagnosis that incorporates the individual—both mind and body—as well as the interpersonal and contextual is crucial to the treatment of sexual dysfunctions from the Intersystems perspective. This chapter begins with a review of the diagnostic criteria for sexual dysfunctions as outlined by the American Psychiatric Association (APA) in the *Diagnostic and Statistical Manual of Mental Disorders,* fourth edition text revision (*DSM-IV-TR*), with etiology and risk factors outlined. Next, we present limitations of and debates surrounding the *DSM* categories as a way to guide clinicians through the complexities of diagnosis. Last, we explain how to provide a multiaxial diagnosis of sexual dysfunction, providing a platform for diagnoses using the Intersystems framework.

Diagnosing With the *DSM-IV-TR*

The *DSM* is the standard classification system in the United States for mental disorders. Published by the American Psychiatric Association, it contains the diagnostic codes clinicians use for communicating among themselves, record-keeping, and insurance reimbursement. Its fourth edition was published in 1994, with a text revision (*DSM-IV-TR*) in 2000. The current role of the *DSM-IV-TR* in sex therapy is to help clinicians make treatment decisions about mental disorders, which include the nature of the problem, identification of other problems that exist along with the sexual problem (comorbidity), expectations for improvement (prognosis), and treatment strategies.

The *DSM-IV-TR* uses the human sexual response cycle model first described by Masters and Johnson (1966) and later altered by Kaplan (1974) to identify a sexual dysfunction. Kaplan's model emphasizes a triphasic sexual response including sexual desire (libido), arousal (excitement), and orgasm. Sexual dysfunctions are "characterized by a disturbance in the processes that characterize the sexual response cycle or by pain associated with sexual intercourse" (APA, 2000, p. 535). Sexual dysfunctions fall into one of four categories:

- disorders of desire: hypoactive sexual desire disorder (HSDD), sexual aversion disorder (SAD);
- disorders of arousal: female sexual arousal disorder (FSAD), male erectile disorder (ED);
- disorders of orgasm: female orgasmic disorder, male orgasmic disorder, premature ejaculation (ED); and
- sexual pain disorders: dyspareunia, vaginismus.

The changes or disturbances in any phase of the sexual response cycle are not absolute or in any way objective (i.e., there is no scientifically derived threshold for diagnoses) but must "cause marked distress or interpersonal difficulty" (APA, 2000, p. 535; criterion B of all 302 diagnoses). To be categorized as a sexual dysfunction, the disorder must not be better accounted for by another Axis I disorder (except another sexual dysfunction) and cannot be due exclusively to the direct physiological effects of a substance or a general medical condition (criterion C).

The *DSM* also has three specifiers for each dysfunction, which aid in clarifying their onsets, conditions, and etiologies. There are three specifier types:

Lifelong or acquired. For the specifier *acquired,* the client must have previously had nonproblematic sexual function in whatever phase of the sexual response cycle in question. For example, a client who had been able to delay ejaculation with previous partners, but is unable to do so with his new girlfriend, whom he finds more sexually experienced and "out of his league," would be diagnosed with *premature ejaculation, acquired.* In acquired sexual dysfunctions, it is important to note the context of onset, such as any changes in physical or mental health, job or relationship status, etc. For sexual dysfunctions to be specified as *lifelong,* the condition must have been present since the client's earliest sexual activity.

Generalized or situational. This specifier indicates whether the dysfunction is global or only occurs some of the time. It refers to whether the client suffers from the problem in every sexual situation, or whether the client experiences the problem in some situations, but not all. Situational sexual dysfunctions suggest a psychological etiology, and here it is important to note whether the sexual problem may be an adaptive response to current or past trauma or stress. For example, a couple may present for treatment because the female partner seems never to want to have sex with her husband. In private, she notes that her lack of sex drive "disappears" in the presence of other men, but that she cannot make herself feel sexual toward her husband, no matter what. The recorded diagnosis would be hypoactive sexual desire disorder, situational, and may serve to keep the couple from gaining a greater sense of intimacy or to avoiding addressing the husband's frequent experiences of erectile failure.

Psychological or combined factors.

Each of the sexual dysfunctions is summarized in Table 3.1.

Limitations of the *DSM* Diagnostic Categories

The *DSM* provides the information necessary to assign a diagnosis that meets insurance or other third-party payer needs; however, it may not provide a full enough understanding of the factors that precipitate, maintain, contribute to, or follow a sexual problem. The *DSM* understands normal sexual functioning to include the capacity to experience desire and satisfaction (that is, receptivity to sexual activity), with the experiencing of orgasm under suitable circumstances (Sugrue & Whipple, 2001). This has led to what some believe is sexology's preoccupation with coitus and orgasm (Tiefer, 2001; 2002). This section reviews some of the limitations of the current *DSM* categories and definitions in order to provide clinicians

TABLE 3.1   *DSM* Classifications

Classification	Disorder	*DSM* code	Diagnosis (from *DSM-IV-TR*) "Persistent or recurrent…"	Differential diagnosis
Sexual desire disorder	Sexual aversion disorder	302.79	Extreme aversion to, and avoidance of, all (or almost all) genital sexual contact with a sexual partner	Substance abuse Menopause Chronic pain Depression—especially feelings of worthlessness or excessive or inappropriate guilt (which may be delusional) nearly every day
	Hypoactive sexual desire disorder	302.71	Persistently or recurrently deficient (or absent) sexual fantasies or desire for sexual activity	Same as sexual aversion disorder
Sexual arousal disorder	Female sexual arousal disorder	302.72	Inability to attain, or to maintain until completion of sexual activity, an adequate lubrication-swelling response of sexual excitement	
	Male erectile disorder	302.72	Inability to attain, or maintain until completion of sexual activity, an adequate erection	

Orgasmic disorders	Female orgasmic disorder	302.73	Delay in, or absence of, orgasm following a normal sexual excitement phase	
	Male orgasmic disorder	302.74	Delay in, or absence of, orgasm following a normal sexual excitement phase during sexual activity that the clinician, taking into account the person's age, judges to be adequate in focus, intensity, and duration	
	Premature ejaculation	302.75	Ejaculation with minimal sexual stimulation before, on, or shortly after penetration and before the person wishes it	
Sexual pain disorders	Dyspareunia	302.76	Genital pain associated with sexual intercourse in either a male or a female	The pain need not be experienced only with sexual intercourse or penetration, women will generally complain of discomfort during gynecological examinations or when inserting a tampon as well Men can suffer from this disorder
	Vaginismus	306.51	Involuntary spasm of the musculature of the outer third of the vagina that interferes with sexual intercourse	

with a better understanding of how sexual problems arise and impact other areas of functioning. Such information is presented to help with a more accurate diagnosis and treatment plan.

Dysfunction Versus Problem

Sexual dissatisfaction is not a diagnosable disorder. However, many of our clients, especially females, report a lack of sexual pleasure, enjoyment, and satisfaction, despite being able to respond sexually in terms of having an adequate sex drive, becoming aroused, and being able to achieve orgasm. A sex therapist may be presented with an individual or dyadic sexual problem that may or may not qualify as a sexual dysfunction in *DSM* terms. Sexual dysfunction implies that normal functioning is impaired and criterion B requires that this impairment cause personal or interpersonal distress. However, we encourage clinicians to consider those sexual problems that clients present with that may not qualify as an Axis I dysfunction, but do produce similar levels of distress. For example a woman may be troubled by what she believes are physical cravings for sexual contact. This could be understood in a number of ways, none of which the *DSM-IV-TR* currently discusses. It could be a case of what some researchers term "persistent sexual arousal" (discussed later) or it could be a case where gender socialization patterns and sexual scripting do not allow the woman to admit her sexual desire. When a woman then has physiological responses or urges, these are "read" by the woman as problematic. Although the *DSM-IV-TR* does not provide an easy category of diagnosis for this type of situation, it is vital that the therapist take seriously the woman's distress.

A far more common sexual problem for which there is no clear axis I diagnosis is incongruent sexual desire or turn-ons within a couple. It is sometimes difficult to determine whether the problem is real or based on a perceived discrepancy. One interesting case involved a woman who said she had HSDD. On further examination, her husband wanted to have sex three or four times a week and she wanted sex one or two times a week. Her level of desire was within normal limits, but she thought that she must always please her husband and should share his level of desire.

Etiology—Physiology Versus Psychology

From the Intersystems perspective, there is a false dichotomy between physiological and psychological causes of dysfunction; criterion C, which requires a psychological or combined etiology, artificially limits our ability to diagnose and treat effectively. For example, erectile dysfunction as a consequence of diabetes or a substance-induced sexual dysfunction cannot be given the 302.72 diagnosis, but they both may produce a profound level of personal and interpersonal discord, warranting clinical attention. Recent studies show that sexual problems with a purely physiological basis are best treated with an approach that combines medical and psychotherapy approaches (Rosen, 2007). In cases where a purely physiological problem is causing a couple distress, the clinician should give a diagnosis of a partner relational problem and proceed with a sexual problem treatment plan, as shown later in Chapter 4. Clinicians may find a high number of cases with a mixed etiology, which the *DSM-IV-TR* does permit. In either case, having as clear and as accurate an understanding of etiology as possible will help the clinician formulate the optimal treatment plan and bring in the appropriate referrals for medical examination and pharmacological treatment.

Comorbidity

Not only are many cases of sexual dysfunction due to a mixed etiology, but it is also true that sexual dysfunctions co-occur with physical health issues, other sexual dysfunctions, and other mental health problems, including substance-related, mood, and anxiety disorders. Although the connection of anxiety disorders, performance anxiety, and premature ejaculation is complex and far from universal, more and more researchers are finding a bidirectional correlation between sexual dysfunctions and depressive, eating, and anxiety disorders as well as physical health problems. Clients may present with a combination of physiological and psychological disorders that are impacting sexual functioning. For example, a woman with breast cancer may experience hypoactive sexual desire, not purely because of her medical condition, but also as a consequence of changes in her own body image brought about by her health status. Here, it is important to view and treat the dysfunction within the context of her health status rather than as independent of it or as a strict and direct consequence of her cancer. Clinicians should review Chapter 7 for a better understanding of how chronic illness and impaired physical functioning can impact sexual problems and specific interventions for such cases.

Clinicians will often see cases in which a client will present with more than one sexual dysfunction or disorder. The *DSM-IV-TR* allows for as many diagnoses as necessary on Axis I, but it is assumed that the first listed is the principal diagnosis. There is no way to indicate the interactional quality of a dual diagnosis. Quite frequently, for example, erectile dysfunction will serve to mask and/or exacerbate male hypoactive sexual desire.* Generally, in such cases, it is important to triage, discern etiology, and attempt to treat the most pressing sexual concern first. Restoring erectile capacity alone may not "cure" the man of a low libido, just as increasing a man's sexual desire without addressing the diminished erectile functioning will only produce frustration. Thus, the interaction of problems must be considered in designing a treatment plan, including all sexual problems in both partners and how they interact with each other.

Individual or Relational Problems

A common presentation is a couple seeking treatment for erectile dysfunction. On the one hand, the problem is clearly an individual one. On the other, the distress the erectile dysfunction causes may be felt by both partners. Another common presentation is an individual seeking treatment for a mismatch in a couple's levels of sexual desire, which is framed as her hypoactive sexual desire. Individually, the woman may report that her sexual drive is fine with her and becomes a problem only in relation to her husband's greater desire for sex. A diagnosis of hypoactive sexual desire disorder may or may not be warranted; however, it is important not to limit diagnosis to an individual disorder. Thus, it is important in diagnosing to ascertain whether the level of distress is personal or relational or both.

Another limitation to an individual diagnosis is that there is frequently comorbidity within the couple. We have observed numerous cases where sexual problems are the consequence of relationship conflict and difficulty. We have also observed numerous cases where the sexual problems precipitated or exacerbated a more general lack of intimacy in and satisfaction with the relationship. In these cases, determining cause and effect of the sexual dysfunction may not be easy, so treating both the couple and the sexual difficulties simultaneously or planning to treat both in a stepwise fashion becomes important.†

---

* Chapters 4 and 5 give details on the assessment and treatment of such comorbidity.
† The section, "Presenting Problem Versus Other Clinically Relevant Problems," in Chapter 5 details how to do this.

Diagnosing relational problems is a central part of developing interventions and treatments from the Intersystems perspective. As shown in the chapter on assessment, the level of severity and degree to which nonsexual aspects of a relationship are disrupted by the sexual problem greatly influence the perception, and hence treatment, of the problem. The *DSM-IV-TR* allows for quasi-relational diagnosis through the V codes, which are ways of noting relationship issues that are either a focus of clinical attention in the absence of other disorders or risk factors for negative outcomes in treatment. Sex therapists will most commonly rely upon the following:

V61.1:   partner relational problem or physical/sexual abuse of an adult;
V61.9:   relational problem related to a mental disorder or general medical condition;
V62.2:   occupational problem;
V62.3:   academic problem;
V62.4:   acculturation problem;
V62.81: relational problems;
V62.82: bereavement; and
V62.89: phase-of-life problem or religious or spiritual problem.

Unfortunately, there is currently no set criteria for any of the V codes, and interpreting when and how to use the codes is left up to the clinician's discretion. As can be seen from the listing, the problems are vague and the categories quite broad, which can be difficult for beginning sex therapists to apply appropriately. A thorough assessment of the individual's dyadic patterns or current couple interactions will help ascertain which V code is applicable and when to use it.

Sexual Problems Not Currently in the *DSM-IV-TR*

The sexual nosology that is used today (*DSM-IV-TR*) is an evolving document. Sexual disorders have never been given much attention in the diagnostic manual. Sex therapy is a relatively new field and new knowledge about how to classify and define disorders is being researched more actively. However, some of the "common" problems identified still do not appear in the classification system. The following sections review some of these problems.

Sexual Compulsivity or Nonparaphilic Hypersexuality

Sexual compulsions mask or can be a symptom of a manic disorder. This problem refers to an excessive involvement in sex with a high potential for painful consequences (e.g., STDs). The distinction between a sexual compulsion and a manic episode is that, in mania, the mood disturbance is sufficiently severe to necessitate hospitalization to prevent harm to self or others (or there are psychotic features), but in sexual compulsion, hospitalization may result as consequence of risky sexual acts or the need to remove oneself from the environment that allows for acting-out.

Female Persistent Genital Arousal Disorder

Female persistent genital arousal disorder is a persistent genital arousal that is not caused by any feelings of sexual desire and that frequently does not diminish with orgasm. In some but not all circumstances, it is accompanied by genital swelling, suggesting a physiological, typically neurological, basis to this newly discovered phenomenon (Leiblum, 2007b). Because of the shame associated with this disorder, it is likely that the prevalence is underreported, but still rare. A validated treatment approach has yet to be discovered, but Leiblum (2007b) reported success in one case via client self-monitoring, massage, and stretching exercises.

Noncoital Sexual Pain Disorder

Noncoital sexual pain disorder is a recurrent pain caused by sexual stimulation not involving coitus (Basson, Berman, & Burnett, 2001). The International Consensus Development Conference noted that a significant number of women experience pain during noncoital forms of sexual stimulation, such as when having their breasts fondled or during cunnilingus. Sexual behaviors and acts outside intercourse are currently not included in the categories of vaginismus or dyspareunia (Hollows, 2007). This new category of problems recognizes that sexual activity need not necessarily involve penile–vaginal penetration. Thus, the category of sexual pain disorder may be more applicable to nonheterosexual men, who may suffer from a form of sexual pain during anal penetration (discussed in Chapter 5).

Multiaxial Diagnosis From the Intersystems Perspective

The sexual dysfunctions are listed as Axis I disorders, but only a multiaxial formulation will give a full diagnostic picture. Following the Intersystems approach will ensure a multiaxial diagnosis and will hone the clinician's instincts to look beyond a client's immediate presentation to consider the interpersonal, intergenerational, and sociocultural contexts of the client's life, including comorbidity, factors that may complicate treatment, and ways the sexual problem may be serving to mask intimacy or other issues in a couple. Multiaxial diagnosis addresses the following five areas:

Axis I: mental disorders
           V codes: relational problems
Axis II: personality disorders and mental retardation
Axis III: general medical conditions
Axis IV: psychosocial stressors and their severity
Axis V: global assessment of functioning (GAF)
           global assessment of relational functioning (GARF)

An Intersystems diagnosis (or one that investigates the individual system, the interactional system, the intergenerational system, and the sociocultural system) will incorporate all five axes of the *DSM-IV-TR*. On Axis I, the clinician will code the relevant sexual dysfunction while noting any personality disorders or mental retardation on Axis II. The clinician should indicate any physical disorders and conditions on Axis III. These three axes can be seen as corresponding to the individual system within the Intersystems approach. When providing a *DSM-IV-TR* diagnosis, the frequency, intensity, and duration of symptoms as well as previous sexual functioning should be addressed to aid in the development of an Intersystems or comprehensive and integrative treatment plan.

Clinicians utilizing the relevant relational V code will begin to address the interactional system, which would include significant refinements to the catch-all "partner relational problem." The ways in which relational processes become intertwined with individual psychopathology generally and with sexual dysfunctions specifically are complex and poorly understood. Although research is beginning, levels of funding are far from adequate and clinical applications have yet to appear that help clarify these interactions. Assessment of the interactional systems will shed light on how emotional contracts, communication styles, and patterns of couple interaction both reflect and reinforce sexual problems. As a minimal measure, clinicians should diagnose any and all relational problems with the appropriate V codes. Additionally, the global assessment of relational functioning (GARF) scale, which can be found in Appendix B of the *DSM-IV-TR*, provides an additional rudimentary diagnosis of the interactional system on Axis V.

Axis IV requires noting significant social and environmental stressors that warrant clinical attention. This axis reflects the intergenerational and sociocultural systems in the Intersystems approach. Messages about sexuality, just like child-rearing, are transmitted intergenerationally and within cultures and subgroups. Sex therapists should ascertain the level of discord regarding sexual messages, attitudes, and beliefs between partners and between an individual and his or her sociocultural environment.

4

Case Formulation

Introduction

The Intersystems approach renders a comprehensive assessment and provides a flexible treatment strategy customized for each unique couple. Far from being overly complex, this approach can be easily managed with the appropriate case formulation. The following format for conceptualizing sexual difficulties is based on the Intersystems case formulation developed by Weeks and Treat (1992). This format for case formulation has three main sections: (1) presenting problem definition, (2) Intersystems assessment, and (3) treatment plan and strategies. Thus, it provides an analysis of the problem and offers treatment strategies examining individual biological, psychological, and intergenerational components; the couple's interactional patterns and dynamics; and sociocultural factors surrounding and impacting the couple. We will review each section of the case formulation template and then using a clinical vignette, giving an example of how to complete the case formulation. An example of the case formulation format is provided in Figure 4.1.

Presenting Problem

As discussed earlier, our fundamental assumption is that every couple is different. Thus, we do not attempt to fit every couple to one model or theory, but rather adapt an all-encompassing approach. The aim of this first section is a succinct understanding of general information about the sexual problem. Most of this information will come during the client's initial phone call, through intake forms, or during the first session. When using a clinical interview to obtain this information, the therapist should be sure to give each partner equal time to talk and encourage each to be as specific as possible. The clinician may not need to ask specific questions at this stage, but will need to be prepared to begin asking specific questions as soon the presenting problems have been clearly defined.

We advise beginning with a general, open-ended question that will get at the variety of sexual problems the couple is experiencing. For example, a statement such as, "Tell me what brings you here today," is usually appropriate if followed up with more probes to gain more specifics. The clinician needs to determine how long they have been having this problem and if they can trace the beginning back to any specific time or event. The therapist asks this and continues to assess whether both partners demonstrate a shared understanding of when the problem began. The couple should be asked about any solutions they have attempted already, including medical and alternative treatments. They may describe a number of attempted solutions, so the therapist should actively search for any sense of hopelessness or despair. Finally, the changes each partner wants to obtain from therapy and how each believes these changes will benefit them, their sexual lives, and their relationship need to be identified. Once the clients have given an overview of the problems as they see them, they should be asked if there are any other sexual problems. Before moving on, the therapist may summarize the problems that have been presented in an effort to make sure nothing is overlooked and ask the couple to rule out other sexual problems.

Developing an Intersystems Case Formulation

For the reader's convenience, we have included a case formulation form at the end of this chapter. The purpose of this form is to assist in conceptualizing the client's concerns. Although this is not the only way that we believe a case can be conceptualized, we find it useful to have specific details about the couple in one place. This form has three sections. The first gathers background information on the couple (i.e., duration of relationship, etc.). The second provides a place for the therapist to delineate the presenting problems. Because there are frequently many problems that accompany a couple's presentation, we advise that each presenting problem be addressed separately. The third section presents a place to provide an Intersystems assessment. Once this document is completed, the therapist can return to it as needed over the course of treatment and have a clear understanding of the couple's progress. See Figure 4.1 for a blank template of the case formulation form.

Chapter 2 provided detailed information on how to obtain a full panel of assessment information and conduct a sexual history. This information should be reviewed before completing the second section, Intersystems assessment, of the case formulation form (Figure 4.1). The goal in the Intersystems assessment section is to organize all of the various assessment data into a clinical picture of what is going on and why the couple is experiencing what they are, and to suggest strategies for treatment based on this particular organization of the clients' information. Next, we briefly suggest what information may be relevant at each level of the Intersystems approach and ways to present it in a clinically useful way.

Individual Systems—Physiological

As mentioned earlier, certain physiological things impact sexual functioning, including:

- diseases (i.e., heart disease, atherosclerosis, diabetes);
- age-related conditions;
- certain psychological disorders with physical components;
- medication; and
- certain lifestyle factors (i.e., smoking, alcohol usage, etc.).

The therapist should ask about the presence of any physical ailments or biologically influenced mental illness the clients describe, as well as a summary of the clients' general health status, which may be obtained through client report or, if permission is acquired, from the clients' physicians. Further, work with the clients to ensure that cardiovascular health, hormonal levels, and neurological function are all adequate to support sexual functioning.

Once all of this information is assessed, the clinician needs to record it within his or her notes and/or the case formulation form. Options the therapist has for treatment at this point include: providing psychoeducation on lifestyle risks—diet, tobacco, drug and alcohol use, exercise, stress reduction; referring for physical exam to rule out a biogenic etiology; and referring to a physician for further treatment if a biogenic cause has already been determined.

Individual Systems—Psychological

The psychological levels of the individual system include psychopathology, mental illness, personality, temperament, developmental stages, sexual values, and overall disposition toward relationships. Once the therapist has adequate information about an individual client's psychological history, he or she must identify how these factors are relevant to the creation, maintenance, and treatment of the sexual problem and reflect them in the case formulation form.

Individual Systems—Family of Origin

The clients' families of origin and early socialization messages surrounding gender, sexuality, intimacy, and bodies can greatly impact how they understand both their own sexuality and the couple's sexual difficulties. This section of the case formulation lists the family-of-origin factors that are interfering with better sexual functioning, such as negative sexual messages, lack of attachment and appropriate modeling of affection in the family, as well as any history of sexual trauma or abuse.

Interactional Components

Rather than noting whether or not the couple has "communication difficulties" or "problems with intimacy," this section of the case formulation form should contain specific concepts from Strong and Claiborn's model that address the systemic aspects of relationships. This includes congruence, interdependence, and attributional strategy (revisit Chapter 1 for further description).

Intrapsychic Components

The three intrapsychic components in this model were discussed at length in Chapter 1: interpretation, definition, and prediction. In sex therapy cases, clients may interpret behavior incorrectly, define the relationship differently, or predict the partner's behavior inaccurately. Each of these may contribute to the sexual problem the couple is experiencing. Such intrapsychic components should be noted and accounted for within the case formulation so that the therapist is sure to include them in treatment.

Further, we described earlier how incongruence can result in or contribute to HSDD. Couples may have an incongruent definition of what constitutes an appropriate frequency of sexual activity or what kinds of sexual activities are acceptable. At this point in the case formulation, the therapist should note whether the couple has congruent definitions of salient behaviors and then provide hypotheses of how to help them reach a consensus.

Interdependence pertains to the extent to which partners depend on one another to meet their emotional and sexual needs; thus, the case formulation form should note the overall level of interdependence that the couple displays. Typically, highly interdependent couples want to stay together, allowing the therapist to exert more pressure and thus proceeding through treatment much more quickly than couples with low levels of interdependence. Sex therapists should be attuned to the couple's interdependence level and should assess their problem definition in light of it because the level of interdependence in the relationship may be bound up with how realistic an appraisal of what successful treatment and the resumption of a satisfying sex life looks like. Couples who are less interdependent may be tentative about the continuation of the relationship and less likely to complete treatment; therefore, this information should be noted on the case formulation form and the therapist should proceed slowly and cautiously.

Attributional strategy is the third interactional component. Generally, the following treatment considerations should be noted in this section of the case formulation form:

- What role did/does each partner play in the creation and continuation of any sexual problems?
- How does each partner define and attribute the sexual difficulty?
- How can the therapist treat the problem in terms of a systems perspective?
- How can the therapist ensure that the therapy is balanced? In other words, the therapist should outline what each partner could gain from the therapy individually, as well as the impact to the dyad.

Society, Culture, History, and Religion

We define cultural context very broadly as everything in the environment that can affect the ability to form a healthy sexual relationship. As norms change, couples should work to understand the extent to which culture and contemporary society have played into their decision-making, values, and behaviors as a couple. Over the decades, values about sexual behaviors such as masturbation, different positions, oral sex, premarital sex, anal sex, mate-swapping, and so on have changed significantly. These need to be acknowledged and noted within the case formulation.

Therapist's Overall Impressions

The sixth and last component of the Intersystems assessment section of the case formulation form contains the therapist's overall impressions. Here, any impressions that may have bearing on the treatment plan are noted. The therapist should be sure to note any factors that may complicate treatment; the prognosis and expected length of treatment, as it exists at this stage of the therapeutic relationship; and ethical and/or professional issues that may influence the chances of a successful treatment.* Fears of rejection may impact the therapeutic relationship if the client begins to see the therapist as a parental figure or savior. Likewise, a client's fears of feelings can complicate treatment in that clients will dissemble around their true feelings, expressing what they believe their partner or the therapist wants them to feel or avoiding any discussion of feelings and focusing too narrowly on sexual knowledge or technical skills.

In short, the therapist must carefully develop a treatment plan in collaboration with the couple that considers the individual (biological, psychological, and intergenerational) factors, the couple dynamics, and sociocultural factors. Once the therapist develops a treatment plan for the therapy, it is appropriate to share it with the couple for their input. Having client buy-in and understanding is crucial and until an agreed upon treatment contract has been reached, the therapist should not presume to treat the couple. The contract may change over time, but having an initial agreement as to the nature of the problem and the path to its resolution is key to success. By having an agreement regarding the treatment plan from the outset, the couple has control (in terms of ownership and responsibility) over their treatment and the therapist has provided informed consent. With these factors in place, it is more likely that the couple will comply with treatment because they will perceive that the therapist is working "with them" rather than "on them." Once a treatment plan is agreed upon,

---

* Factors that complicate treatment include the battery of fears surrounding intimacy discussed in Chapter 6.

the therapist may let the clients review the plan, sign it, and place it in their chart. Of course, they know the plan may change or evolve as treatment unfolds. Thus, there is a constant process of collaborating with the client in changing the course of treatment.

INTERSYSTEMS SEX THERAPY CASE FORMULATION FORM

Partner A name: _____   Age: _____Gender: ___ Male ___ Female
Partner B name: _____   Age: _____Gender: ___ Male ___ Female

Type of Relationship:
___ Married   ___Dating (not cohabitating)
___Cohabiting   ___Other _____
___Same Sex Union   Length of Relationship: _____

Reason for referral:_____
_____
_____

PRESENTING PROBLEM

Give a concrete problem description including onset and duration of each problem, attempted solutions, clients' beliefs about why the problem exists, and changes desired from each partner's perspective.

Problem Description Partner A:

Problem Description Partner B:

Onset and Duration:

Attempted Solutions:

Desired Goal:

Figure 4.1a   Case formulation form.

INTERSYSTEMS ASSESSMENT

1. Individual systems—Physiological

2. Individual systems—Psychological

3. Individual systems—Intergenerational system

4. Interactional system

5. Sociocultural system

THERAPIST'S OVERALL INITIAL IMPRESSIONS

- *Factors that may complicate treatment*

- *Prognosis and expected length of treatment*

- *Ethical and/or professional issues that may exist*

Figure 4.1b   Intersystems Assessment.

5

Treatment Principles, Strategies, and Techniques*

Introduction

Assessment and treatment are overlapping processes. Once the therapist has a basic understanding of the problem and its onset, duration, and impact upon the couple, it is a good idea to proceed immediately with specific treatment strategies and continue deeper assessment as he or she works to alleviate distress and instill hope. Too much initial history taking may cause the couple to lose interest in treatment and to think therapy is answering questions without being offered any solutions. As the treatment proceeds, the therapist can always (and usually will) obtain new information about the presenting problem as well as new problems that usually emerge. While working with the couple, the therapist can probe for information about one problem while another issue is being concurrently treated. The key is the therapist's ability to shift back and forth appropriately between assessment and treatment.

The *goal of treatment* is the overarching concept that drives treatment or what it is that successful treatment should provide. The strategy is the general method the clinician uses to implement the treatment; it should derive from the same theoretical understanding of the problem used in goal development. Also, the techniques are the specific interventions used to implement the strategies. Sex therapists need to address individual, couple, and sociocultural factors that contribute to a couple's sexual problems; therefore, they will need to rely on a variety of treatment approaches and theoretical perspectives. Unlike strictly behavioral approaches, the role of

* Written with Amy Ellwood, University of Nevada School of Medicine.

the partner is considered in the creation, continuation, and correction of the problem. The treatment is always balanced in the homework so that each receives some kind of emotional, affectional, sensual, or sexual pleasure.

Beginning Treatment

This guide is useful when time and experience are limited in beginning with a new client. As soon as possible, the therapist should follow up by gaining more information from the resources listed so that he or she can offer effective treatment.

Initial Phone Call

The initial phone call is the therapist's first contact with clients. Most sex therapy is conducted on a fee-for-service basis. Thus, the therapist wants to return the client's call as quickly as possible and spend a few minutes on the phone gaining some information and making the appointment. In our practice, clients have reported that a previous therapist did not call them back, called them back days later, or was in a hurry on the phone. These are all recipes for losing the client. There are many ways to let the phone conversation unfold, but we have found that the following basic steps work well. The therapist should:

- ask the caller if he or she has 5 minutes to talk in private over the phone;
- ask how the caller got the therapist's name;
- ask about the nature of the problem, stating that he or she wants to make sure that the caller is beginning with the right therapist; the caller should be allowed time to describe the problem briefly;
- ask if the caller has seen a physician or another therapist for this problem. If so, the clinician should tell the caller that he or she would like to hear what happened and perhaps talk with the treating provider or see the records. The therapist should explain that although he or she may or may not need them, records from other providers can only be released with the client's permission;
- request that the caller bring a list of medications and dosages to the first meeting;
- ask if the caller is married or has a partner and explain that sex therapy works best when both partners come to the sessions. The clinician can

ask whether the partner is willing to come and, if not, then this can be discussed in the first session;

- explain hours, fees, location, etc.;
- ask if the caller would like to set an appointment and make an appointment if the caller is ready. If not, the therapist should ask if there is any way in which he or she can help the caller; and
- ask if the caller has any questions.

The fact that the therapist takes 5–10 minutes to talk with the person on the phone indicates his or her interest in working with the caller. Rarely does any provider spend this much time doing an initial phone screening. Callers immediately appreciate the attention or service they receive from the initial contact.

The Initial Session

The initial session is one of relationship building and discovery. In sex therapy cases, most clients are ashamed, embarrassed, uncomfortable, or have some difficulty talking openly. The therapist can open the session with a statement that he or she knows the couple is coming in to improve their sexual life and knows that getting started is difficult for most clients. The therapist can ask the couple (assuming the couple is the unit of treatment) how they feel about coming to therapy for help with a sexual problem. The therapist can normalize the feelings, if appropriate, and work to help the couple become more comfortable. The therapist may explain that, in most cases, the couple needs to be seen together; however, if there is a need for some individual sessions or work and everyone agrees to the plan, the therapist may see one or usually both individually. If the therapist chooses to conduct some individual sessions later, the rules of how to do so and the rules of confidentiality have been carefully described by Weeks, Odell, and Methven (2005). Once the couple appears ready to proceed with an assessment of the problem, the therapist can begin.

The Triage Tree

Although the treatment of each of the problems described in the next section involves making complex decisions of what techniques to use in treating specific sexual difficulties, it is essential to know the sequence in which the problems are treated. Research informs us that the presentation of a solitary sexual dysfunction is rarer than may be first understood. Multiple sexual problems may exist within the individual and within the couple (Michael, Gagnon, Laumann, & Kolata, 1994). Thus, the clinician must make decisions about which problems to treat first and how to work with problems concurrently.

We have generally found that the decision-making principles presented here work to ensure effectiveness of any technique by providing a logic of when to begin treating a specific dysfunction and how to triage comorbidity both within an individual and within the couple system. Of course, not every couple will present with the same constellation of problems, so the therapist needs to understand the underlying logic more than the specific ordering. In general, we suggest the triage options for the following situations: (1) presenting versus other problems that warrant clinical attention; (2) comorbidity (the effect of all of the client's illnesses, not just the presenting problem) in an individual with desire or an interest in having a sexual relationship always taking priority, and (3) treating multiple sexual dysfunctions in the couple. See Figure 5.1 for a representation of the decision-making processes.

Presenting Problem Versus Other Clinically Relevant Problems

In many cases, more than one presenting problem warrants clinical attention. We have found that it is best to treat the presenting problem first. This is true unless any of the following exist:

- *Medical problems or medication-induced sexual dysfunction.* The biogenic component of any dysfunction must be addressed first before commencing relational sex therapy. Although medical intervention is first required, full resolution of the biomedical issues is not necessary before some preliminary sex therapy can be commenced. The couple should be told that progress will be limited during this phase, but that relational sex therapy is foundational to resolving their sexual problems fully, especially in terms of preparing the couple to regain sexual intimacy. During this time, the therapist should complete the client's sexual history, prescribe some bibliotherapy, and work on improved sexual communication and other issues.
- *Severe individual psychopathology.* Untreated mood disorders and substance abuse are just two examples of individual psychopathology that

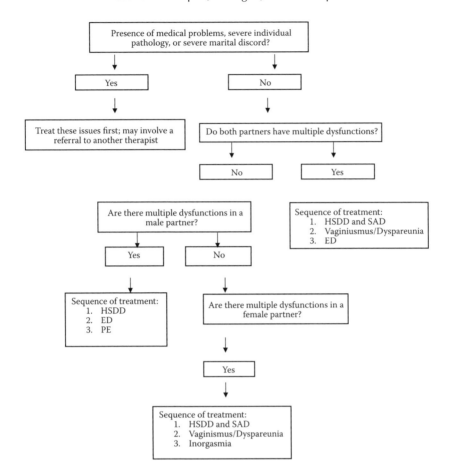

Figure 5.1 Triage tree.

will limit any form of sex therapy. In these cases, the sex therapy must be delayed while the individual issue is treated.

- *Severe marital discord.* Severe marital discord, such as domestic violence, is contraindicated in all types of sex therapy. In these cases, therapy should focus on the couple's relational dynamics, moving only to sexual issues when there is a strong enough relational foundation for the two individuals to become sexually intimate with each other.

Note that in establishing a system for triage, an understanding of levels of severity is vital. In cases of moderate individual pathology and couple discord, it may be possible, even preferable, to conduct the sex therapy. The litmus test in distinguishing between the two is whether the couple can successfully begin the exercises assigned to them. Additionally, some therapists may want to refer the couple to another therapist to treat individual psychopathology or for conflict management issues. The couple needs to understand that progress will be much slower when individual and couple issues are interfering with beginning sex therapy or when they fail to understand or agree with the treatment plan.

Multiple Dysfunctions in an Individual

The general sequencing of treatment for men follows the following decision tree: (1) hypoactive sexual desire, (2) erectile dysfunction, and (3) premature ejaculation. We believe that it is best to approach comorbidity in an individual from the idea that desire is paramount. A man with little desire will not be interested in the other two problems. If he suffers from premature ejaculation, he will need to be able to achieve an erection of sufficient quality in order to work on the premature ejaculation. Of course, as one problem is being solved, it may be possible to phase in work on the next problem in the sequence.

Likewise, the general sequencing of treatment for women is (1) hypoactive sexual desire and sexual aversion disorders, (2) vaginismus and dysparenuia, and (3) inorgasmia. A woman with no desire will probably not be interested in treating any of the other sexual problems. Women with sexual pain disorders may have a number of issues around fear of pain and anxiety that interfere with becoming orgasmic. However, with some women, the treatments can overlap after the initial fear of sex and anxiety have been overcome.

Co-Relational Sexual Dysfunctions

No matter what combination of dysfunctions is present in the couple, it is imperative to treat multiple sexual dysfunctions in the couple systemically. The general sequencing of treatment when both partners have sexual problems is more complex than in individual cases. Therapists will have to weigh not just the number of problems and the types, but also the severity of the issues and the couple's readiness to engage in overlapping treatment. In many cases, work can begin with both partners and proceed up to a point where one partner must move forward before the other can proceed. For example, in treating a couple where the male has erectile dysfunction and the woman experiences inorgasmia, the man will need to be able to sustain an erection during intercourse prior to working with the woman on having coital orgasms. Treatment, then, should begin with him and move to increase her sexual awareness as he gains erectile capacity; the goal is that when both are ready, intercourse is possible. The general sequencing of treatment for couples is

1. hypoactive sexual desire and sexual aversion disorders;
2. vaginismus and dysparenuia;
3. erectile dysfunction; and
4. other dysfunctions.

Again, the hypoactive sexual desire is treated first. Partners with HSD are generally not interested in working on any other problems in themselves or the other. Vaginismus is usually the second problem that needs attention, if it is present. The woman's fear and anxiety will make it difficult to work on any other problem in her own sexual functioning, let alone her partner's. Erectile dysfunction would be the next problem in the sequence. Without an erection, the man cannot work on premature ejaculation. Likewise, the treatment of his partner's sexual problems may be limited if there is no possibility of intercourse and his performance anxiety is negatively impacting the couple's sexual dynamics.

Some dysfunctions can be treated concurrently. For example, premature ejaculation and inorgasmia can be treated concurrently up to the point where the female client begins working on coital orgasms. As the duration of coitus increases in the treatment of premature ejaculation, more opportunities for brief intercourse can occur. However, in order for the woman to work on having coital orgasms, the male partner will need to be able to sustain intercourse to a duration that meets the needs of the female. Thus, timing and sequencing of homework are very important when addressing multiple sexual dysfunctions in a couple.

Keeping Treatment Systemic

In the section that immediately follows, we lay out specific treatment plans for the sexual dysfunctions. We remind the reader that some problems are treated concurrently with a partner's sexual problems. These may directly overlap or be somewhat sequential. Throughout the process, we are looking for ways in which the partner may be contributing to the problem in the identified client, including ways in which the partner might sabotage treatment.

The following treatment sections only focus on the partner with the problem and what to do for him or her. Our general principle is that, in every exercise, the experience should be balanced so that the partner is not simply a surrogate therapist, but rather derives some pleasure from the experience that is defined. We discuss this issue further in Chapter 9 as well as in Hertlein, Weeks, and Gambescia (2008). Sometimes, partners can have sexual experiences during the homework and, at other times, it might be limited to time together, affection, or something sensual. Obviously, a woman cannot ask for intercourse from a man being treated for erectile dysfunction, but she might ask for affection or oral sex leading to orgasm. The therapist needs to (1) ensure that the partner always feels the experience is reciprocal and receives something he or she wants, and (2) make sure during the session that what the nonidentified partner would like is possible and will not interfere with the therapeutic programs described next.

Keeping the treatment systemic has to be a priority. One way to accomplish this goal is to be purposeful in developing the treatment plan. Figure 5.2 presents a sample template that may be helpful in treatment planning. A therapist who chooses to use elements in this table must be certain that the plan reflects equal focus on both partners.

Treatment of Specific Sexual Dysfunctions

Many of the strategies and techniques of sex therapy seem very simple and straightforward. However, our experience in supervising clinicians over many years has shown us that the clinician must not only know which technique to use when, but also *how* to use it. Implementation is crucial to effective sex therapy and can only be learned through further reading, extensive practice, and supervision. This book is not designed as a substitute for any of these three criteria. Clinical supervision by an experienced, preferably certified, sex therapist is essential for beginning sex therapists.

Hypoactive Sexual Desire

Hypoactive sexual desire disorder (HSDD) is the most complex of all problems to treat because so many factors may contribute to the lack of desire, thus making it difficult to outline a specific course of treatment.

SAMPLE TREATMENT PLAN

Intersystem Area	Vulnerability	Treatment Plan	Specific Techniques
Individual Biological			
Individual Psychological			
Dyadic			
Family of Origin			
Sociocultural			

Figure 5.2   Treatment planning grid.

An individual may have never felt desire, may have a lack of desire for only his or her established partner, may have felt desire at one time but lost it, or may feel desire for no person. Clients who have never felt desire and have no desire for desire are by far the most difficult to treat. Generally, they come to treatment at the urging of their partner or as a result of their guilt toward their lack of desire. The principle of treatment is to identify the factors suppressing desire and remove them through the appropriate treatment modalities and strategies while promoting factors that enhance sexual desire.

Strategies and Techniques
With some disorders, the treatment plan is fairly standardized—do step one first, then step two, and so on. Hypoactive sexual desire requires a great deal of flexibility on the part of the therapist. We will present an outline of treatment roughly based on our books (Hertlein et al., 2008; Weeks & Gambescia, 2002). Assessment is key in determining how treatment is approached. Depending upon the factors present that suppress desire, the order of some of the following treatment steps may need to be altered.

Provide bibliotherapy and education. The couple needs general information about sexuality and specific information about the nature of the sexual problem. Specific strategies are more fully described in Chapter 11.

Overcome pessimism and skepticism. Most couples presenting with HSDD have had the problem for some time and wonder whether talking about the problem can ever make it better. The therapist needs to inquire about their level of commitment to the relationship because, in our experience, HSDD can lead to severe marital disruption and, in some cases, divorce. The issue of their potential hopelessness needs to be addressed and the therapist needs to provide them some information that will instill hope. It is imperative that the therapist has a hopeful attitude.

Reduce the impact on the relationship. The partner may be feeling frustrated or angry and, in some cases, think that the HSDD partner is deliberately withholding sex. The therapist needs to assess the impact on the relationship, educate the couple, and discuss other ways they can connect emotionally, affectionately, sensually, and in some limited ways sexually, if possible.

Reduce response anxiety. Response anxiety is a term used to refer to the anxiety experience over not feeling enough or any desire, not feeling desire quickly enough or often enough, and not feeling enough or any desire in "sexual" contexts. For example, a woman might suggest making love on a particular night and the man with HSDD might begin to feel anxious that he is not going to bring enough or any desire to the evening's plans. Couples need to be educated that response anxiety is nearly universal in cases of HSDD. Of course, the therapist should verify whether one or both do in fact feel response anxiety. If so, they can be educated about what it is and what it does. Response anxiety is part of the cycle that suppresses sexual desire even more. The HSDD partner anticipates a sexual encounter, feels anxious, and, in turn, the anxiety lowers the ability to feel desire. The therapist gives the HSDD partner permission to feel only the desire he or she feels and not to try to force himself or herself to feel more desire. The therapist may also use thought-stopping to try to stop the thoughts creating the anxiety. For example, if the HSDD partner is thinking, "I must feel more desire to please my partner," he or she will only end up feeling less desire. In another example, the client might be thinking that he or she can only be attracted to someone with red hair because of an early past relationship. The client can use thought-stopping to control this idea and experience the desire he or she would otherwise have for the partner were it not for this thought.

Conduct cognitive work. Earlier in this chapter, we mentioned that sexual desire and sexual inhibition of desire are mirror images. Their negative sexual thoughts are collected during the assessment phase. During treatment, the therapist works with these thoughts in several ways. The overall strategy is to develop thoughts that counter the negative thoughts as well as develop positive sexual thoughts. Of course, when the negative thoughts are reviewed with the couple, the first decision to be made (with the couple's help) is which thoughts are just unfounded negative thoughts and which ones represent the need for a real change in the sexual/couple relationship. For example, if the thoughts "we fight all the time" or "he never shows me any foreplay and is rough and abusive sexually" were part of the list, the therapist would first want to conduct couple therapy to work on changing the sexual behavior. Cognitive changes could be directed toward unfounded thoughts. For unrealistic, unfounded, irrational, or distorted thoughts, the therapist will want to help the HSDD partner find one or more neutralizing or counter thoughts and develop a list of positive thoughts. The positive thoughts should be in the categories mentioned earlier of self, other, or partner, and relationship and should include multiple thoughts. The therapist may recommend that the positive thoughts be rehearsed every day until they become second nature.

Define oneself as a sexual person. In our experience, many HSDD clients do not see themselves as sexual beings. As long as this is true, they are not going to have any sexual feelings. Thus, we developed a technique known as the *"Sexual Bill of Rights"* (Weeks & Gambescia, 2002). The therapist asks the client to write about himself or herself as a sexual being and to describe what he or she is entitled to feel sexually, to experience, to receive, and to give. Most clients present a weak statement at first and are asked to work on strengthening the statement over the course of 3 or 4 weeks or until they are able to develop a strong sense of their sexual entitlement.

Increase sexual fantasies. In the definition of HSDD, the idea that sexual fantasies are missing from the HSDD partner is a key element. However, we have seen no treatment programs of HSDD that include the use of sexual fantasies. The primary function of sexual fantasies is to increase a person's sexual desire or to help maintain desire (Loren & Weeks, 1986). The therapist should ask about whether the HSDD client has sexual fantasies and to what extent. If fantasy life is nonexistent or very low, the therapist can discuss the importance of increasing both thoughts and fantasies. The client needs to be given permission to have fantasies and discuss the meaning of fantasies in the context of his or her relationship and personal belief system. Books, magazines, tapes, and other materials may be used to help prime the client to develop a few fantasies to use when he or she wants to feel or increase the level of sexual desire.

Reframe. Reframing is a strategy used to change the meaning of a problem or situation, usually from something viewed as negative to positive and from individual to systemic. In the case of reframing sexual problems, a variety of techniques can be used (Weeks & Treat, 1992). In some cases, the therapist may want to reframe the HSDD as a couple's problem, if that is the case. For example, the therapist might say:

> Your wife is the one who lacks sexual desire, but both of you have underlying fears of intimacy that motivate you to find some symptom to keep you from becoming too emotionally connected. At the present time your wife/partner, Mary, is the one manifesting the symptom and protecting the two of you from having to deal with your underlying fears.

Work with fears of sexual intimacy. The sexual fears of intimacy are the same as the underlying fears of intimacy (as described in Chapter 6 and also in Weeks & Treat, 1992b; 2001). These fears include such phenomena as fear of exposure, control, anger, rejection, and abandonment. We have described this work extensively in the books mentioned earlier. The therapist will need to spend a considerable amount of time identifying each underlying fear and then helping the client understand its origin and function and how to move past the fear. All the underlying fears of intimacy have the potential to disrupt sexual functioning.

Assign appropriate homework. Homework must be tailored for HSDD couples. A couple of common homework exercises use sensate focus to help the couples reconnect physically, but not in a sexual way. We described a new approach to sensate focus that should be used in our prior book (Hertlein et al., 2008). Another homework assignment that is often used is called 'nondemand intercourse' (Kaplan, 1974). Nondemand intercourse is intercourse that does not make a performance demand (in the sense of any performance, including response anxiety), so the person with HSDD does not feel any pressure. Other assignments that we have developed, such as learning how to create a sexual environment, creating seduction rituals, and becoming more egosyntonic (more comfortable) with sexuality, can be used.

Erectile Dysfunction (ED)

This section describes the treatment of psychogenic ED. However, a therapist may also play a useful role when the problem has an organic basis and is being treated medically. More and more cases are also of mixed etiology; as the baby boomers are growing older, organic impairment and psychogenic problems are intermingled (Weeks & Gambescia, 2002). The principle of treatment is to lower performance anxiety and fear while creating small successes toward having an erection.

Many advances have been made in the treatment of ED in the past decade (Hertlein et al., 2008; Leiblum, 2007a; Weeks & Gambescia, 2000). It is now known that as men grow older the chances of medical problems and increasing medications, especially blood pressure medications, can interfere with erectile ability. Thus, it is important that men have had a physical examination by a physician or more specialized evaluation by a urologist who is well trained in treating sexual dysfunction. Men may have the problem for strictly organic reasons, psychogenic reasons, or mixed etiology. The following questions help the therapist begin to understand some of the fundamental causes. A thorough description of causes and assessment has been described in Weeks and Gambescia (2000). Although the history-gathering questions are covered in greater detail in Chapter 2, some beginning questions would include:

- Are you taking any medications? If so, which ones?
- When did you last have a physical and were there any problems?
- Have you seen a urologist for this problem?

- When did you first notice a problem with your erections?
- Did your problem begin suddenly or gradually?
- How has your erectile ability changed over time?
- What is it like today? What percent of the time can you get a good erection?
- Can you maintain a good erection with masturbation?
- When you attempt intercourse, at what point do you begin to lose the erection? Can you get it back if you lose it?
- Do certain positions work better than others in keeping the erection?
- When you get an erection, do you rush to have intercourse?
- Do you try to will yourself to have a strong erection? What happens when you do this?
- What thoughts do you now have about being able to keep an erection? Do you feel anxious about losing it?
- How do you and your partner react when you lose your erection?
- Has this problem led to avoiding sex with your partner?
- What kinds of things have you tried to overcome this problem?
- What is your theory about why you are having this problem?

Strategies and Techniques

Provide bibliotherapy and education. Psychoeducation for men with ED might include information about the impact of psychology and physiology on sexual health.

Dispel myths about erections. One of the most common myths a man has is that in order to have sex he must have an erection. This myth, along with others, should be challenged. The most important information is that a couple can have satisfying sex without a full, firm erection or with no erection at all. Another concern that men have is that just talking about having an erection will not enable them to have an erection. The therapist describes the process so that the couple understands how the therapy is going to accomplish the goal. The men need to know that an essential part of treatment is not talking but rather carrying out specific homework assignments with their partner.

Dissipate performance anxiety. Masters and Johnson (1970), Kaplan (1974), and Weeks and Gambescia (2002) have all described the significant role that performance anxiety plays in ED. The formula is quite simple and should be described to the couple; as anxiety and fear about performance (getting and keeping an erection) increase, the ability to perform decreases significantly. Men get caught in a vicious cycle of performance anxiety. The loss of an erection produces anxiety, which in turn makes getting an erection more difficult, which increases anxiety.

Two techniques are useful in reducing performance anxiety after the man knows about the detrimental role it plays. First, we never actually prescribe that the client should achieve an erection. The wording of the exercises is "if it happens." Second, we ask men to place themselves in a mental loop of focusing on the here and now and on what is feeling good right now and what they would like in order to keep themselves feeling good. We explain that any time they start to think about the next moment or past experiences they are inviting the anxiety back. Men can become cognitively distracted with a myriad of thoughts that interfere with keeping an erection. These thoughts might be "it never works," "I don't want to fail again," "my wife must hate having sex with me," and so on. Some researchers have called this problem cognitive interference. It seems to us that the difference is largely semantic. Men with performance anxiety think "awful thoughts"—the same as men who experience what is termed cognitive interference.

Conduct cognitive work. Men with ED often have a number of negative thoughts about their erectile ability that generate the fear and anxiety. The therapist should identify negative thoughts and help men to neutralize those thoughts. The therapist should also check for thoughts that suggest deeper psychological causes. ED is usually the result of performance anxiety and just treating this anxiety may produce significant improvement. However, the therapist must also listen for deeper causes of ED, such as lack of desire for the partner, individual psychopathology, fear of pregnancy, and a host of other reasons described by Weeks and Gambescia (2002).

Use adjunctive treatment. Men who have had ED for a long period of time or have severe cases can be treated with the simultaneous use of oral medications such as Viagra, Levitra, or Cilias or, in more severe cases where there is more neurological involvement, an injectible treatment such as Caverject. This gives them confidence and better erectile ability while they pursue the exercises. There have even been some case reports of men who used an ED medication, regained confidence, and were able to discontinue the medication without therapy.

Assign appropriate homework. A number of homework exercises are typically used in treating ED. The therapist should always keep in mind that the partner should be getting some emotional or physical pleasure while she is helping the man with the exercises. The following homework assignments are based on sensate focus. The first exercise is a whole body caress with no genital stimulation; the man is told that there is absolutely no expectation of getting an erection. Once his performance anxiety is lower, they can move on to genital stimulation just for the purpose of discovering what feels good. He should be told again there is no expectation of an erection and to use a dry hand for stimulation. As the man's performance anxiety decreases and he regains touch with his genital sensations, the stimulation can become more focused and lubrication can be used for more extended periods of stimulation.

At this point, the man is probably getting an erection. He is told not to hurry things but to enjoy getting the erection slowly and not to worry if it disappears. At some point, the man is able to obtain an erection on a consistent basis. Once he has gained erectile consistency, he is told to do something that he usually perceives as unusual: to ask for stimulation and, if an erection occurs, to keep it for a while and then to stop the stimulation in order to lose the erection. He repeats this experience three times before he is allowed to ejaculate (if that is desired). The lesson he learns is that if he loses an erection during a sexual interaction he will be able to regain it. Finally, he is told that he should only ejaculate with a full, firm erection; otherwise, he is reinforcing his ED.

Another homework assignment that is given later in the treatment of ED would be brief penetration. Once the man is confident that he can obtain an erection, the couple is asked if they would like to try a penetration exercise. If they are ready, the therapist prescribes the following. The female partner prelubricates so that penetration is easy and they work out how penetration will occur. Usually, it works best if she stimulates him while he is on his back. When he is erect, the woman briefly mounts him for a few seconds and then goes back to manual stimulation. This procedure is repeated a number of times, with the length of penetration becoming more and more extended. The man needs to be told that physically moving his body around and interrupting physical stimulation reduces his chances of keeping an erection. Men will sometimes get an erection but then "fumble around" trying to find a position for intercourse, lubrication, etc. and lose their erection. Older men generally need constant stimulation to the point of penetration.

Prescribe free-form intercourse. The couple has now learned enough to be able to move on to intercourse without specific instructions. They are reminded that, if there is a problem, to use the preceding strategies and techniques to help them. If they had been using a medication, the dosage has gradually been reduced to nothing or to the lowest dose possible because there is the possibility of some organic involvement.

Once the couple has completed the assignments, the therapist needs to help prevent relapses by monitoring progress, especially the return of performance anxiety. Every week he or she should ask the man about his level of performance anxiety about having sex and especially about having an erection. If performance anxiety begins to increase, the clinician may need to review the techniques to maintain control over anxiety.

Premature Ejaculation (PE)

PE is the inability to control when ejaculation occurs. We believe the best goal for the treatment of PE is to have ejaculatory control. Time to ejaculation no longer becomes an issue because the man is able to delay ejaculation for as long as he likes and as long as his partner likes. PE is probably one of the simplest sexual problems to treat. Men with PE have a very low threshold of stimulation needed for ejaculation. In treating PE, the female partner must do much of the work; therefore, it is important to keep the idea of her receiving emotional and physical pleasure in mind when she is on the receiving end of the homework assignment.

PE is one of the most common problems found in men (Michael et al., 1994). Many men with PE can only delay ejaculation for 2 minutes or less after penetration. The principle of treatment is to enhance the man's ability to control when he ejaculates (or has an orgasm) by raising his threshold of stimulation.

Strategies and Techniques

Assign the squeeze technique. In cases where PE is about 2 minutes or less during intercourse, we begin with the squeeze technique as described by Masters and Johnson (1970). In our experience, men with less ejaculatory control benefit from the squeeze technique first and then graduate to the start–stop technique. Men who have more control may begin with the start–stop. The squeeze technique is applied to the tip of the penis by squeezing from top to bottom with a firm squeeze for 2 or 3 seconds or until the ejaculatory urge dissipates. The partner provides stimulation with a dry hand and, when the man feels he is about to ejaculate, he says, "Squeeze," and the partner applies the squeeze. The squeeze automatically inhibits ejaculation. They repeat this process at least three times during a single session and can have as many sessions during the week as they like.

No lubrication is used in the first exercise or so. Stimulation should be slow and little pressure applied at first; over time, more rapidity and pressure are applied. The man is allowed to ejaculate at the end of the exercise. Once the man is able to delay ejaculation for a longer period of time, the therapist switches to the start–stop technique as described by Kaplan

(1974). The partner starts and stops stimulation, giving the man time to recover from being overstimulated. The partner will provide stimulation and, when the man feels that he is ready to ejaculate, he will ask her to stop. He takes a break long enough for the urge to ejaculate to subside and then she repeats the process. The same schedule described before is used in this and the following manual stimulation exercises. Then, once the man has achieved some degree of control with dry hand stimulation, they can switch to using lubrication in order to better simulate the vaginal environment. We recommend using Albolene cream (unscented) because it does not dry out and is of the right viscosity. This product can be obtained at www.drugstore.com or in most drug stores.

Introduce the "quiet vagina technique." Instruct the couple to repeat the preceding exercises using lubrication until the man can successfully delay ejaculation 10–15 minutes with a few starts and stops. Once the man feels he has gained good control with manual stimulation, the couple can move on to a very defined method of intercourse. The partner provides manual stimulation to erection. She prelubricates with a copious amount of lubrication in order to reduce friction. (We recommend almond oil, which is massage oil found in health food stores; it is very slippery, thus reducing friction.) Once the man has an erection, the woman mounts from on top and does not move. Masters and Johnson (1970) called this the "quiet vagina" technique. He is allowed to become accustomed to intravaginal stimulation without ejaculation. For physiological reasons, most men can control ejaculation better when on the bottom.

The quiet vagina technique is repeated several times with slowly increasing stimulation or movement. The man must monitor his sensations carefully and let his partner know when to stop or slow down. Once control is achieved using the female-superior position, the man can try different positions. He is to monitor his sensations and slow down or stop when needed. She is to use plenty of lubrication. Over time, his control will improve. The more they practice the techniques, the more quickly the results are obtained. The therapist constantly monitors their progress. The couple may need to slow down or proceed faster through these exercises. Sometimes they may need to go back to some earlier exercises. The therapist should check to make sure the man is monitoring his sensations and telling his partner what he needs. Some men with PE have no idea when they are about to ejaculate. Masters and Johnson called this a lack of premonitory sensations. The sensations are always present, but these men fail to recognize the cues. An essential part of all the exercises described is to develop an acute awareness of these sensations so that the man can "pace" himself during intercourse.

We have found that women generally report enjoying short, deep strokes when working on their orgasms. In contrast, men often think they need long strokes throughout intercourse. Men should be taught to use the short, deep strokes while using the coital alignment techniques (see, for example, Estronaut, 1999). By keeping the tip of the penis deep inside the vagina, the friction or stimulation is minimized, as opposed to longer strokes, whereby the penis passes over the PC muscle surrounding the vaginal opening. The coital alignment technique is described in the next section and is for the benefit of the woman.

Inorgasmia

Inorgasmia refers to the inability to reach orgasm during manual stimulation (such as with a vibrator, hand, or oral stimulation) or to the inability to achieve orgasm via intercourse (coital inorgasmia). Heiman, LoPiccolo, and Palladini (1988) have written about this problem for many years from a psychoeducational and behavioral perspective. Hertlein et al. (2008) discuss the problem from an integrative perspective. Although inorgasmia may have an organic basis, it is most commonly an issue of lack of experience with masturbatory orgasms and other psychological factors.

There are different variations of inorgasmia. Some women have never had an orgasm; others have had an orgasm but are no longer able to reach orgasm. In other cases, some can have an orgasm with manual stimulation, but not with intercourse. Again, we assume that inorgasmia is psychological and not the result of a medical condition or drug side effect.* Of course, this assumption is not always true; thus, an assessment of medical factors is required. The treatment program we will describe can be used for a range of women but should be tailored for each particular woman. The steps we will describe are based on the books published by Heiman et al. (1988) and Barbach (2000). Of course, we add the Intersystems piece in our treatment.

Additionally, we do not define inorgasmia as the inability to achieve orgasm with intercourse. We view coital orgasms as an option that a woman may choose or not and that some women may not have the sensory

---

* In some cases, inorgasmia can be the result of taking an SSRI (selective serotonin reuptake inhibitor).

threshold needed to reach orgasm with the minimal amount of stimulation that intercourse affords. The principle of treatment is to work through any psychological barriers to having an orgasm and systematically create enough stimulation for orgasm to occur consistently and then lower the threshold of orgasm to the lowest point possible.

Strategies and Techniques
Explore meaning and barriers to orgasm. The therapist should explore the meaning of having or not having an orgasm with the woman and the couple. Are there negative associations to having an orgasm, such as losing control or being dependent on the partner? What, if any, are the psychological barriers to having an orgasm and working through those barriers? Does the man believe he has to "give" the woman an orgasm because that is his role? Is it a control or power issue? The therapist needs to explore the couple's dynamics around orgasm. Are there couple-related problems that would prevent an orgasm, such as anger or resentment? The clinician should work through the couple-related problems. Also, it is necessary to explore messages in the family of origin and culture. Many women have received negative messages about their sexuality. Asking the client about the messages and conducting a sexual genogram can help uncover these negative messages. One of the most common negative messages is about self-stimulation or masturbation, thus preventing any experimentation that facilitates orgasm with a partner. (Self) masturbatory training is one of the most important factors in a woman becoming orgasmic.

Provide bibliotherapy and education. The bibliotherapy for inorgasmia should include information on sexuality in general, a book on becoming orgasmic, the experience of masturbation and orgasm, and sexual fantasies. The therapist may wish to consult Komisaruk, Beyer-Flores, and Whipple's (2006) book, *The Science of Orgasm,* which contains information about the latest in orgasm, neuroanatomy, neurotransmitters, etc.

Assign appropriate homework. The homework exercises initially involve just the woman learning about her body and how to stimulate herself to orgasm. The partner does not need to be involved unless the woman wants him present. The majority of women in our experience are more comfortable doing these exercises alone. The behavioral assignments are carried out on a three-times-per-week basis. Later, the man will be providing her with stimulation, so she is to provide him with whatever form of stimulation that feels good for him (except intercourse) to which they mutually agree. Remember that the therapist may accelerate or decelerate these steps or skip some entirely, depending upon the presentation of the couple.

The therapist should begin the process of giving homework assignments keeping the preceding steps in mind throughout.

First, the woman or couple should do a genital examination with a mirror and book in order to identify all of the sexual parts. The genital examination will help the woman become more comfortable with her genitalia, improve communication, give the couple the language to discuss what needs to be stimulated, and assure the woman that she has all the parts. The woman should touch the genital area just to find out what parts feel like and which parts are most sensitive. Any resistance to touching the genital area should be processed. The woman should be asked to touch the genital area in order to produce pleasurable sensations. The goal is not orgasm, but rather to discover the pleasure-giving parts. The therapist should tell the woman to focus on the clitoral areas and her reactions and feelings should be processed. The woman should be asked to touch the clitoral area in order to produce as much pleasurable sensation as possible but told not to worry about orgasm. She should be asked about what she felt and her reactions and feelings processed. The therapist should continue to ask this question for the subsequent exercises up to intercourse, but not prescribe an orgasm.

If the woman is feeling pleasurable sensations, then she should move on with increased stimulation.* Some women will unconsciously cut off the sensations and thereby not be able to reach orgasm. The therapist can prescribe 10–20 minutes of self-stimulation, starting with slow, soft stimulation in the beginning and moving to harder, faster stimulation later. He or she can suggest that the woman use a lubricant to avoid irritation. Hopefully, this will trigger an orgasm or move her close to an orgasm. This exercise can be repeated a few times if the woman feels she is approaching an orgasm. If manual stimulation alone is not enough to produce an orgasm, then more intensity is needed. The use of a vibrator such as the Pocket Rocket, Turbo Rocket, or other high-quality vibrator (which can be purchased at a variety of sexual Web sites as well as Amazon.com or www.goodvibes.com) can be prescribed for external stimulation. The clinician should explain the rationale for using a vibrator and ask how the woman feels about using one. He or she should explain how to use the vibrator—for example, apply to the clitoral area, using varying degrees of pressure, and if the stimulation is too intense, wrap a cloth around it to reduce the intensity.

Using a vibrator almost always produces an orgasm within the first week of prescribing the assignment. The therapist should process the

---

* If she is not feeling sexual sensations, there is clearly a psychological barrier that needs work.

sensation of orgasm, how long it took, and how the woman felt about using the vibrator. He or she should prescribe the use of the vibrator until the woman can achieve an orgasm quickly and consistently with this method. When orgasm consistency has been reached, the use of the vibrator can begin to be phased out. The woman should use the vibrator until near orgasm and then switch to manual stimulation. The use of the vibrator should be phased out earlier and earlier so that the woman can eventually have an orgasm through manual stimulation alone.

The partner may become involved at any point around these steps, depending on the woman's desire. The couple then repeats some of the same steps with the man providing the stimulation. The man now is to provide the manual stimulation with the woman giving instructions. She is to focus on what is feeling good in the moment and what she wants to keep it feeling good. The clinician needs to explain the need for stimulation of sufficient duration (10–20 minutes), focus (clitoral), and intensity (how much pressure and rapidity of movement) and to focus on facilitating communication and the man's willingness to cooperate. Is he doing things to sabotage the exercises? Eventually, the woman should be able to achieve orgasm with her partner providing the stimulation. This may take several exercises and, if needed, they can repeat the preceding exercises with the male using the vibrator and then fading it out.

Once the couple has reached a point where the woman can easily achieve an orgasm with manual stimulation, they are ready to move on to intercourse under prescribed conditions. The therapist should make sure that they feel ready to move to the next step. The partner provides foreplay or stimulation to near orgasm. The couple quickly switches to intercourse, with female on top. With female in the superior position, she can press the clitoral area into his pubic area, thus maximizing stimulation. This procedure is called the coital alignment technique. This exercise is repeated a number of times to see if she can learn to have an orgasm this way. Some women do not prefer to be on top. The male-superior position can also be used with the coital alignment technique (Kaplan, 1992). The male thrusts deeply and with short strokes, pressing into the female's pubic/clitoral area to maximize stimulation.

A technique that can be used before or after is to have the man provide manual or vibrator stimulation during intercourse with the woman in the superior position. After a few sessions, it will become clear whether the woman can achieve an orgasm only with manual stimulation, vibrator, or oral sex; needs extra stimulation with intercourse; or cannot have an orgasm though intercourse, with or without additional stimulation. The therapist processes whatever the woman is capable of doing and how the couple will incorporate her orgasmic potential into their lovemaking. It is important that the couple feels that they have succeeded in achieving sexual satisfaction even though the goal of coital orgasms may not be met. Any final issues that may have been overlooked earlier can be discussed at this time.

The therapist can discuss the overall pattern of lovemaking and how they can maximize their pleasure with each one's capabilities, levels of desire, pattern of initiation, frequency, and so on. Although not part of treating inorgasmia, the therapist may also choose to help the woman learn to become multiorgasmic through the use of combined G-spot stimulation and clitoral stimulation (Kahn, Whipple, & Perry, 1982).

Vaginismus

This disorder is one in which the woman has difficulty with penetration because the muscle surrounding the vaginal opening tightens up or goes into spasm. Historically, vaginismus has been viewed as a psychogenic disorder involving the pubococcygeus (PC) muscle surrounding the vagina tightening so that penetration is difficult, if not impossible (Leiblum & Rosen, 1989). Women presenting with vaginismus should always be evaluated first by a gynecologist who is familiar with pain disorders and their proper evaluation. Generally speaking, women with vaginismus will present with a sensation of stretching, burning, or tearing around the vaginal opening. Pain that is deeper, pain that is not localized in the vaginal opening, or a sharp, well-defined pain that is highly localized usually represents a medical problem that may have been missed by the physician. Thus, it is crucial for the woman to be evaluated by a physician who is well trained in the evaluation of all pain disorders related to intercourse or penetration. The therapist may refer the client to a urogynecologist, who can identify sexual pain disorders. Urogynecologists do residencies in urology and gynecology; the therapist can consult the American Urogynecologic Society at http://www.augs.org/ for more information or http://www.mypelvichealth.org/ to find a physician and tools for patients.

Assuming the problem is vaginismus, treatment consists of several well-defined steps. Some women do not have severe vaginismus, so they may skip a number of the initial steps. The principle of treatment is to facilitate the relaxation of the PC muscle so that penetration is comfortable.

TABLE 5.1   Disorders Web Sites

Topic/Web site	Web address
Female dyspareunia	http://www.vulvodynia.com.au/info/terminology.html
V-views	http://www.vagisil.com/special_200609.shtml
Vulvodynia.com	http://www.vulvodynia.com/
Vulvar vestibulitis	http://www.uihealthcare.com/depts/med/obgyn/patedu/ vulvarvaginaldisease/vestibulitis.html

Women with vulvodynia, vestibulitis, vestibulodynia, and clitorodynia need a different approach to treatment. The clinician unfamiliar with these disorders may confuse them with vaginismus and begin a course of treatment based on PC relaxation, which is inappropriate. Although sex therapists do not often see these disorders, the therapist should be able to differentiate them from vaginismus and have some idea about treatment. The therapist can consult the websites in Table 5.1 for more information or Hertlein et al. (2008).

For these problems, the therapist may help the couple adapt their sexuality to these conditions and help the woman with the chronic pain and change in sexual image.

Strategies and Techniques
Vaginismus not only is a disorder with a physical component, but also creates fear that can be of phobic proportions. Almost all therapy programs to date, with the exception of Meana (2006), fail to address this concern. The therapist needs to ask about the level of fear of penetration.

Provide reassurance. The first intervention is to reassure the woman that the treatment will be pain free because she will always be in control of when penetration occurs and in control of the penetration. Women with this disorder often refuse to seek treatment until they are desperate to have a child or their partner is threatening to leave them or have an affair.

Reduce the impact on the relationship. The impact on the relationship should be discussed early in treatment. The partner's frustration, anger, and other feelings need to be explored or they may reveal themselves in inappropriate ways. For example, one client reported that her boyfriend occasionally made flip remarks about how sexually frustrated he was. Such remarks negatively impact communication and impair trust. Additionally, the male partner may have a sexual problem or have an unconscious need for his partner to be unable to have intercourse.

Explore the meanings. The therapist needs to explore what this problem means to the woman. Some couples have never been able to consummate their relationships, and this is very distressing to them. Others refuse sex and see themselves as bad wives or defective. Additionally, although most treatment approaches focus on the behavioral, the therapist needs to explore possible causes for the problem, such as sexual trauma or sex-negative messages in the family. These need to be worked through prior to the therapy beginning unless the client would like to begin doing homework exercises and work on the issues. If homework is attempted and the client fails to carry through on the homework, it is possible that her fears and anxieties are too strong for her to begin.

Assign appropriate homework exercises. To begin the homework, the woman is instructed to make time to do her homework and get relaxed prior to starting. She is instructed to try to insert one very well lubricated finger very slowly and with no pain. She is to stop when resistance is experienced, allow the muscle to relax, and try to insert more. In the first few exercises, insertion may be minimal or just involve challenging the pubococcygeus muscle. The woman is to focus on relaxing the muscle and may read, listen to music, or watch TV while doing the exercises with herself. Some women will use the bathtub for a setting. Once she can insert one finger comfortably, the woman then moves the finger in and out, which challenges the pubococcygeus muscle. Once the woman can insert one finger comfortably and move it in and out, she is to do the same exercise again but try to insert two fingers, beginning with one and then the second. Then, when she can insert two fingers with no movement and no pain, she begins to move two fingers in and out.

The woman can now bring her partner into the exercises. She can have him watch her demonstrate the progress she has made or move to the next exercise. The man is instructed that his role in the couple exercises is to provide a stiff finger. They must agree that she is always in charge of the penetration exercises. She is to lubricate herself well and hold his finger while inserting it slowly. The preceding exercises are then repeated with the male partner: one finger, no movement; one finger, movement; two fingers, no movement; two fingers, movement. Some women can do these exercises fairly quickly; others will take more time. The level of fear usually increases sharply when the partner is involved, so there may be some difficulty, which requires backing up in the sequence of exercises. It is absolutely essential that they both understand that they should not attempt intercourse until told to do so.

The couple is now ready to transition to intercourse. They start with the man inserting two fingers with movement. This is done slowly and with the woman always in control of the process. When she feels ready, she moves on top and very slowly inserts his penis as much as she is comfortable. Eventually, she will be able to insert his penis fully. When this occurs, she is to remain still—no movement—in order to relax the PC muscle. Once she feels ready, she begins to add movement while he remains still. This exercise is continued with more and more movement until the problem is fully resolved and a variety of positions can be enjoyed.

During the last phase of the treatment of vaginismus, men want to move and have an orgasm. The therapist must insist that the woman is in control until the problem is resolved and the woman needs to understand that the man will need stimulation to reach orgasm in most cases or else his frustration and anger will become a problem. During this phase of therapy, the woman may stop at some point because the muscle has not yet fully relaxed and stimulate the man manually to orgasm. During the early phase of treatment, if the digital penetration exercises are not proceeding as outlined, the woman should be referred to a physical therapist for specialized treatment for other muscles that are involved in the pain or to a gynecologist for further evaluation. We advise that the therapist also consult *The V Book: Doctor's Guide to Complete Vulvovaginal Health* by Elizabeth Stewart and Paula Spencer (2002).

The treatment of the sexual disorders reviewed in this chapter is done within the context of the Intersystems approach. Note that the treatment protocols we have outlined are generic and must be tailored for each couple. The techniques are deceptively simple. They do not always work as intended; proper implementation is just as important as knowing the right strategy or technique to use. Adherence to the Intersystems approach and experience will help the beginning therapist learn what to treat when (using our decision trees) and how to implement the techniques effectively. Supervision by a certified sex therapist is an invaluable tool in learning to do sex therapy effectively, and readers are referred to Chapter 11 for information on how to obtain quality sex therapy supervision. Implementation and experience play such a critical role. It is well known that patients who need liver transplants, for example, do much better when they receive surgery from a doctor and his team who do these surgeries on a very consistent basis. Therapists who practice sex therapy must not only receive training, credentials, and supervision, but also be committed to making sex therapy a major component of their practices.

Treatment Concerns of Gays and Lesbians

The general issues of primary importance in the treatment of sexual problems with gays and lesbians are heteronormativity and internalized oppression. Heteronormativity (defined as the belief that heterosexuality, including opposite-sex attraction and "penis–vagina" intercourse, is normative or standard, and the marginalization or punishment of people who vary from heterosexual practices) may impact the client's psychosocial experiences as well as the therapist's comfort, knowledge, and skill in addressing the needs of sexual minority clients and couples. Internalized oppression may impact the client's ability to seek and accept assistance in overcoming any sexual difficulties because of his or her own internal beliefs about what is right and the sexual pleasures to which he or she is entitled. Internalized oppression may also impact how the client sees the nature of the sexual difficulties—particularly attribution strategies—and he or she may feel more responsible for any couple discord than individuals without such feelings of shame.

The specific considerations of sexual minority individuals and couples presenting for treatment include seeking help for problems with:

- lack of knowledge in same-sex sexual practices;
- HIV status discrepancy;
- anodyspareunia (painful receptive anal intercourse); and
- discrepancy in levels of desire or practices desired.

Although sexual orientation plays a major role in the context of a sexual difficulty, it is important to pay attention to other client variables as well. Heterosexual therapists, especially, need to keep in mind that a sexual minority's sexual orientation may not be the defining feature of his or her life and that, along with sexual orientation, it is important to pay attention to the client's age, race, religion, educational level, and social class. Each of these variables plays an important role in how the individual understands his or her sexuality and responds to treatment efforts. However, it is important to note that all sexual minority clients are seeking services within a larger cultural framework of discrimination and nonacceptance. Therapists must strive to understand the ways in which prejudice, discrimination, and violence may have impacted the client's sexual function, as well as his or her general mental health (Bettinger, 2001; Bigner & Wetchler, 2004).

In considering a diagnosis of a sexual dysfunction in sexual minorities, the therapist needs to understand the heteronormativity inherent in the *DSM* criteria. As mentioned in Chapter 3, the sexual pain disorders may overlook both gay and lesbian concerns. Sexual pain disorders are defined as "recurrent or persistent genital pain associated with sexual intercourse" (APA, 2000, p. 556). This definition overlooks the fact that lesbians do not engage in sexual intercourse, but may experience pain upon other forms of stimulation or penetration. Further, the definition overlooks pain that gay men may experience with anal penetration, known as anodyspareunia (Rosser, Short, Thurmes, & Coleman, 1998), which is addressed later.

Additionally, in terms of heteronormativity, Bettinger (2004, p. 70) states that inaccurate views on the part of the therapist may affect a sexual minority client's presentation and the therapeutic process. The therapist's knowledge about gay and lesbian practices and awareness of his or her own countertransference issues are the most important elements in successfully treating same-sex clients. The American Psychological Association (APA) has issued guidelines for working with gay, lesbian, and bisexual clients, but the American Association of Sexuality Educators, Counselors, and Therapists (AASECT) and the American Association for Marriage and Family Therapy (AAMFT) have not. More information is provided regarding these guidelines in Table 5.2. These guidelines place emphasis on therapists actively learning about GBLT issues and cultural concerns and providing referrals when clinicians are practicing outside their level of expertise or have unexamined issues of homophobia of their own that are negatively impacting the therapeutic alliance.

TABLE 5.2   Guidelines for Psychotherapy With GBLT Clients

Guidelines for psychotherapy with lesbian, gay, and bisexual clients American Psychological Association, 1994
Attitudes toward homosexuality and bisexuality
Guideline 1. Psychologists understand that homosexuality and bisexuality are not indicative of mental illness.
Guideline 2. Psychologists are encouraged to recognize how their attitudes and knowledge about lesbian, gay, and bisexual issues may be relevant to assessment and treatment and seek consultation or make appropriate referrals when indicated.

Guideline 3. Psychologists strive to understand the ways in which social stigmatization (i.e., prejudice, discrimination, and violence) poses risks to the mental health and well-being of lesbian, gay, and bisexual clients.

Guideline 4. Psychologists strive to understand how inaccurate or prejudicial views of homosexuality or bisexuality may affect the client's presentation in treatment and the therapeutic process.

Relationships and families

Guideline 5. Psychologists strive to be knowledgeable about and respect the importance of lesbian, gay, and bisexual relationships.

Guideline 6. Psychologists strive to understand the particular circumstances and challenges facing lesbian, gay, and bisexual parents.

Guideline 7. Psychologists recognize that the families of lesbian, gay, and bisexual people may include people who are not legally or biologically related.

Guideline 8. Psychologists strive to understand how a person's homosexual or bisexual orientation may have an impact on his or her family of origin and the relationship to that family of origin.

Issues of diversity

Guideline 9. Psychologists are encouraged to recognize the particular life issues or challenges experienced by lesbian, gay, and bisexual members of racial and ethnic minorities that are related to multiple and often conflicting cultural norms, values, and beliefs.

Guideline 10. Psychologists are encouraged to recognize the particular challenges experienced by bisexual individuals.

Guideline 11. Psychologists strive to understand the special problems and risks that exist for lesbian, gay, and bisexual youth.

Guideline 12. Psychologists consider generational differences within lesbian, gay, and bisexual populations, and the particular challenges that may be experienced by lesbian, gay, and bisexual older adults.

Guideline 13. Psychologists are encouraged to recognize the particular challenges experienced by lesbian, gay, and bisexual individuals with physical, sensory, and/or cognitive/emotional disabilities.

Education

Guideline 14. Psychologists support the provision of professional education and training on lesbian, gay, and bisexual issues.

Guideline 15. Psychologists are encouraged to increase their knowledge and understanding of homosexuality and bisexuality through continuing education, training, supervision, and consultation.

Guideline 16. Psychologists make reasonable efforts to familiarize themselves with relevant mental health, educational, and community resources for lesbian, gay, and bisexual people.

Sexual Ignorance Among Sexual Minority Clients

Gay and lesbian clients presenting for treatment may simply lack knowledge about same-sex sexual practices. Typically, these clients will be less acculturated into the same-sex sexual culture, just having come to terms with their sexual orientation (i.e., they are newly "out") or experiencing their first same-sex relationship. Some ignorance may stem from a lack of same-sex practices visible in the larger society, particularly mainstream media. Gays or lesbians may not know how to engage in parallel behaviors to those shown by heterosexuals on television and the movies, where people frequently learn how to perform sexual acts. Knowledge of such things as how to put a condom on a partner or various sexual positions for mutual genital stimulation may be missing. Other forms of ignorance may involve sexual myths, such as "lesbian bed death"—the belief that sexual activity diminishes in long-term lesbian relationships, which has been shown to be inaccurate (Meana et al., 2006). One client who recently started to experiment with gay sex was ambivalent about any type of anal stimulation because of his fear of AIDS. Once he was educated about safer sex, he was able to enjoy this activity without fear.

HIV Status Discrepancy

As HIV and AIDS become more of a chronic disability rather than an acute, terminal illness, couples composed of one HIV-positive partner and one HIV-negative partner are increasingly common to see in treatment. One issue that may face these couples is how to manage a chronic illness within the couple's dynamics, which is little different from any couple presenting with distress surrounding one partner's diabetes or heart disease. Of course, diabetes is not contagious, and HIV is spread through an exchange of human fluid, particularly through sexual contact. This means that gay couples must be educated about safer-sex practices. Some of these practices are included in Table 5.3. Additionally, Gay.com has a series of safer-sex fact sheets, an STD risk chart, and slideshow as well as a regularly updated safer-sex Q & A section on its website.

One of the interesting obstacles HIV discrepancy presents clinically is the fact that, in some relationships, the HIV-negative partner ignores the

TABLE 5.3   Safer-Sex Practices

Area	Specific practices
Condom use	Using a new condom in every act of anal and oral sex Opening the package carefully (not with the teeth or scissors) Checking frequently during rigorous thrusting to make sure the condom has not broken Holding firmly to the base upon withdrawal Pinching closed and discarding promptly and properly
Oral sex	HIV-positive partners should not ejaculate into their partner's mouth HIV-negative partners should avoid performing oral sex if they have cuts or sores in their mouth, a throat infection, have recently undergone dental work, or have just brushed or flossed their teeth
Anal penetration	Wearing a latex glove during manual penetration of the anus Using a dental dam or clear plastic wrap when "rimming" or orally stimulating the anus, although rates of oral–anal contact transmission are low
Fluid exchanges	"Golden showers" or urinating on bare skin should be avoided by using plastic wrap or PVC suiting Urine, blood, semen, and fecal matter should not come in contact with the eyes or mouth
Sex toys	Condoms should always be used on dildos, "butt plugs," or other sex toys All toys and devices should be washed in warm soapy water before and after use Toys should not be shared with multiple partners Care needs to be taken when using certain types of lubricants on silicone-based sex toys

risk or has an unconscious need to become HIV-positive. Also, as treatment advances increase the ability to live with the virus and feel quite healthy, the positive partner adheres less to safer sex practices. Another issue of concern may be the perception that the HIV-negative partner has more sexual opportunity outside the relationship. This perception may affect larger issues such as sexual fidelity and commitment. Lastly, it is important for clinicians to be sensitive to the stigma faced by HIV-positive individuals in some gay subcultures and the larger culture. Such stigma may produce feelings of shame and guilt that are best treated psychodynamically before attending to the sexual issues that may extend from the stigmatization (Catalan & Meadows, 2000).

Anodyspareunia

Although large-scale studies of sexual minority sexual practices are lacking, two recent studies note the prevalence of anodyspareunia, or pain with anal penetration. Between 12 and 14% of men who have sex with men reported pain during anal intercourse (Damon & Rosser, 2005; Rosser et al., 1998). This pain often was experienced during the men's initial sexual experiences onward and across all sexual situations of anal intercourse, meeting the *DSM* features and specifying criteria of a lifelong, generalized sexual pain disorder. Factors associated with a greater amount of pain experienced in anal intercourse were depth and rate of thrusting, lack of social comfort with gay men, being more "closeted," and less concern over becoming old or unattractive as a gay or bisexual man. Men with anodyspareunia reported that psychological factors were the primary contributing cause of their pain, most notably not feeling relaxed (Damon & Rosser, 2005). As such, treatment should focus on ensuring that the couple uses adequate lubrication, engages in sufficient sexual play (foreplay) to ensure relaxation, and penetrate the anus with one or two fingers or a small, slender dildo prior to penile or hand penetration.

Role and Practices Discrepancy

Gay or lesbian clients, like many heterosexual clients, may present for therapy because one individual wants to engage in certain sexual practices and the other does not. Discrepancy in sexual roles or practices may be more common among gay or lesbian clients because same-sex sexual practices have not become culturally normative, such as intercourse is among heterosexuals (Underwood, 2003). Studies show a tendency for greater role flexibility and exchange in same-sex couples, but this lack of set sexual scripting may be perplexing and confusing to some couples (Bettinger, 2004). Gay or lesbian couples may indicate that one partner's desire to be in a position of either always getting or giving sexual pleasure is causing distress. "Stone-butch" lesbians, for example, may always want to be in the position of giving their partners sexual pleasure and may express strong desire never to have their breasts fondled or be penetrated by their partner. Their partners may in time come to feel as though they are insufficient as lovers or object to the lack of exchange within the couple.

One of our clients presented with her problems in feeling sexual toward her partner. Initially, she began the relationship happy to be the one giving her partner sexual pleasure, but grew resentful when the partner never wanted to reciprocate. This resentment was channeled into a lack of sexual desire. More typically, gay men may come to resent their partners who always want to be in a subordinate position. Referred to as "do-me queens," these individuals may want, or be perceived by their partner to want, only and always to be the object of sexual activity. They do not want to be the partner who is performing actions such as fellatio, rimming, or manually stimulating his partner. Frequently, resentments or disappointments with other areas of the couple's relationship, such as who is responsible for childcare, etc., will be projected onto or highlighted by the sexual discrepancy. Treatment will need to focus on how the partners can reach some consensus regarding their sexual roles and the meaning of these roles for the relationship. Some partners may want to change their ability to engage in certain sexual behaviors.

6

Factors Complicating Treatment

Sexual Misinformation

As part of the Intersystems approach, the therapist has to be knowledge-able about a variety of dimensions (individual, couple, family of origin, etc.) that can complicate the sexual picture for a couple. Unfortunately, these dimensions can also be affected by a number of factors. One such factor is sexual misinformation. Masters and Johnson (1970) stated quite simply that the lack of sexual information contributed to sexual problems. The problem, however, is a bit more complex than stated by Masters and Johnson. Some of the information perpetuates the myths and complicates the problems a couple might have. Although society's interest in sexuality may appear widespread, media and literature portray myths about sex. Further, what prevents people from uncovering accurate information may be their fears and embarrassment about the topic or specific myth.

As an example, Klein (1997) discusses the role that myths and misin-formation play in maintaining the sexual problem in cases of hypoactive sexual desire disorder; in these cases, couples may believe that there is a way that a man or woman should operate, or may be misinformed as to how physiology changes over time. Peterson and Peterson (2007) outline several specific cases of sexual myths, including sexual myths regarding age, anatomy/physiology, sexual performance, pregnancy/postpartum, STDs, sex offending, same-sex attraction, people with disabilities, sex therapy and sexual medicines, and masturbation. For a more detailed dis-cussion on this topic, see Peterson and Peterson.

Further, sexual myths and misinformation lead to a secondary prob-lem: increased anxiety and sexual guilt (Mosher, 1979). Newer studies (see, for example, Bancroft & Janssen, 2000) show that underlying anxiety in people with sexual dysfunction results in faulty cognitions, thus promoting more anxiety (Rosen, Leiblum, & Spector, 1994). In the accompanying volume (Hertlein, Weeks, & Gambescia, 2008), we have shown how anxiety is related to a variety of sexual disorders. In clinical practice, we also see how guilt restricts the expression of sexual feelings and behaviors and have provided ways to address this throughout this guidebook. It may be the case that specific sexual myths are more related to one type of problem than another or to one type of dysfunction, but research has not examined this possible relationship. Therapists, then, need to address the misinformation with couples (Klein, 1997) and consider pairing the strategies for correcting misinformation with anxiety-reducing strategies.

Fears

There are many ways in which a therapist might become aware that fears are impacting the course of treatment. In some cases, clients will not complete the homework assigned to them. Although this might happen on occasion in any treatment, repeated noncompletion of homework after several types of homework assignments might signal to the therapist that there is an issue preventing further growth. Additionally, some couples will miss appointments or attend scheduled appointments so erratically that it is difficult to move forward when sessions are spent reviewing what has transpired within the last few weeks. Because of the nature of sex therapy and the momentum gained from the assignments each week building on one another, it is imperative that the therapist address attempts to sabotage treatment. An effective way to do this might be to discuss with the client the factors or fears that prevent other couples from completing treatment as prescribed. It is important to normalize that these fears come up and that they are part of the process of treatment rather than an indication to stop. Specific fears and how to manage them are detailed next.

Fear of Intimacy

Hertlein et al. (2008) stated that, in general, couple therapy must be completed or at least well under way prior to attempting sex therapy. One area where couple work is important prior to sex therapy is dealing with underlying fears of intimacy because they make it impossible to achieve too much intimacy. Sexual problems are often an expression of one or more of these underlying fears. Without removing or diminishing the intensity of these fears, progress in the couple's sexual relationship will be limited. In fact, in most of the cases that we have treated, the couple cannot make any progress in sex therapy until some work has been done on these fears.

Sternberg (1986) defined intimacy as the sense of closeness, feeling of being connected or bonded, sense of welfare for the other, high regard for the other, trustworthiness, emotional support freely given to the other, etc. The literature has a large body of theoretical and empirical/assessment work on intimacy (Weeks & Treat, 2001b). Unfortunately, most of it lacks any clinical utility. Weeks (Weeks & Hof, 1987; Weeks & Treat, 2001b) developed the idea that a great deal of couple/sexual pathology results from problems in the area of intimacy. Moreover, what sometimes appear to be problems in the areas of commitment and passion are often directly linked to or result from problems in the areas of intimacy. For example, the person who is labeled as being commitment phobic is often reacting to an underlying fear of intimacy that makes it difficult to commit.

The assumption of Weeks and Treat's (2001b) theory regarding intimacy is that everyone who enters a relationship brings with him or her some underlying or unconscious fear of intimacy. For most partners, these fears are not that powerful, so they do not result in severe or disturbing relational and/or sexual problems; however, in other partners these fears can exert a destructive force in the general relationship and also in the sexual relationship. This concept of intimacy as a root cause of marital or sexual pathology is consistent with Sternberg's model of love and was developed over the course of many years in working with couples in sex therapy. It would be impossible to catalog all the possible underlying fears of intimacy. Fortunately, a few of these fears are fairly common and will be described here with an example of how each fear might impact the couple's sexual relationship or lead to sexual problems.

One of the most common fears in sexual dysfunction cases is fear of intimacy. This fear is characterized by several dimensions. A description of the fears as well as a discussion of the implications the fear has on the relationship is summarized in Table 6.1.

Fear of Anger

Some partners are afraid of their own anger or being the recipient of anger from others, especially the partner. The suppression or avoidance of anger

TABLE 6.1   Fears of Intimacy

Underlying fears of intimacy	Description	Implications for the relationship
Fear of rejection/ abandonment	Usually grounded in one's family of origin; perhaps parents ignored, rejected, or abandoned their child. This fear manifests in the adult child's intimate relationships.	The individual will avoid being close or intimate with his or her partner.
Fear of dependency	A fear of becoming controlled or reliant on someone else. Can result in a loss of autonomy, self-control, and independence.	Acts as if he or she does not need anyone and makes every effort to maintain his or her independence. Sexually, he or she will avoid intimacy that shows any needs or vulnerability.
Fear of anger	A fear that one will lose control over his or her anger and hurt another or that anger will be expressed toward him or her.	Not hearing a partner's anger can result in impaired communication or avoidance of discussion of intimate topics; not expressing one's own anger verbally may prevent the development of intimacy.
Fear of feelings	The most common cause is one's family of origin having an excess of out-of-control feelings or being devoid of feelings.	This can result in an avoidance of feeling anything; thus, any intimate contact would be avoided.
Fear of losing control	The fear has two levels: (1) that someone else is going to take control of him or her, and (2) that there will be a loss of self.	Due to culture's strong belief that our body is our own and that we should have control over our sexuality, sex is an area where these fears are commonly manifested.

leads to turning off this feeling and as a consequence turning off many other feelings. They also notice that when they are interacting in an intimacy relationship, conflict and anger inevitably arise. Once they see this connection, they begin to seek the suppression of all feelings and deeper interactions because of the anticipated negative consequences. Because sex is one way of interacting intimately, they may begin to avoid sex. Sometimes, they see sex as an area where they may be criticized or where their feelings may be aroused and anger may surface.

Rich was a man who had recently lost all sexual interest. The therapist ruled out any medical issues, but found that he was experiencing post-traumatic stress disorder from the Vietnam War, where he was a sniper, and that early in life his anger was out of control. If he became angry with someone, he was able to start a physical fight and harm the other person. He entered the Army early and learned to channel his aggression more appropriately. Further, Rich married someone who could vacillate between being passive and aggressive. He could relate to the passive side, but felt anger when she was assertive. The therapist realized that Rich was probably carrying a good deal of anger and resentment toward his wife. After some extended probing, the therapist was able to confirm that this was exactly the case.

The bottom line was that his anger and resentment were also suppressing his sexual interest. Rich needed to do some family-of-origin work, deal with his PTSD, and work on viewing anger and conflict as healthy and productive rather than destructive. His change in his sexual behavior had also followed a failed business where he was angry with himself for not making the business work. The therapist had multiple issues to manage with Rich in individual therapy before he was ready to begin working through the impact of these issues with his wife.

Fear of Feelings

Some partners actually have a fear of feeling their own feelings. Many of them had the experience of seeing feelings that were out of control in their family. In one case, a woman watched her father suffer from bipolar illness, which affected his mood and, consequently, affected her desire to control every aspect of her life. Several other clients reported seeing parents who were feeling depressed much of the time. Others may have seen two parents whose moods led to disengagement or habitual conflict. The message that these children internalized was that feelings eventually only have bad consequences, so it is better not to feel at all.

Anthony suffered from such a fear. He presented to therapy with an inability to reach orgasm. The therapist realized that an orgasm is an intense emotion and Anthony's demeanor was to avoid expressing any feelings. The therapist did a genogram with Anthony and learned that his mother was bipolar. He grew up in fear of her irrational moods and could remember that he made the decision that feelings would never rule his life. Thus, he began to turn off all feelings. He lacked sexual desire but still had sex out of obligation. He wanted to be a good husband, but could not release his feelings through the experience of orgasm. The therapist helped Anthony understand his mother's illness, how he had reacted to her and interpreted her behavior, and how the fear of feelings had continued into adulthood, affecting his choice of a partner and how he expressed himself sexually.

Fear of Losing Control

Losing control has two meanings in a relationship. The first is simply being told what to do by the partner or being controlled behaviorally. When this situation occurs, the partner often fights back and there is overt conflict in the relationship. The second and deeper meaning occurs when one person tries to dictate how the other is to "be." In other words, the partner tries to dictate feelings and thoughts, often in an indirect way that is frustrating to the partner receiving the messages. Partners who receive these messages may have a very weak ego and may select partners who have a propensity to dictate. In other words, individuals with weaker egos may desire to be told how to "be" at an unconscious level, but also may feel the need to rebel against the mandate. This particular dynamic is common in cases of hypoactive sexual desire. Anyone can have mechanical sex or go through the actions, but to feel the desire for sex is a personal matter that another cannot control. The lack of desire for sex is a metaphor for maintaining control over at least one aspect of one's life.

Marilyn and Oscar presented with hypoactive sexual desire disorder (HSDD) on Marilyn's part. She said she would sometimes have sex with Oscar because that was his duty, but she had never really felt the desire for sex after a few weeks into the relationship with Oscar.* The therapist began to explore Marilyn's history and found that she was the "good kid" in the family. When asked why she was the good kid, she talked about her parents pressuring her to conform to how they wanted her to be and how they would strongly disapprove of any act that went "against" them. Marilyn had never been encouraged to develop her own sense of self or autonomy. She believed she was simply an extension of her parents, always trying to please them to gain love and approval. She also tried to please Oscar, but chose her sexuality as the one place where she was not going to lose herself.

---

* When HSDD is present from very early in a relationship, the relationship is usually the more common factor, but in this case, the individual factors were also a priority.

The therapist worked with Marilyn to get her to understand how her parents had not supported her ego development. She needed to move past the belief that the only way to gain love was to please others all the time. The therapist used a combination of family-of-origin work, insight, and cognitive therapy to accomplish these goals. The therapist also helped the couple understand their dynamic and why Oscar had chosen a partner who would never challenge him. Finally, Marilyn was strong enough to allow herself to feel desire and own it without feeling that it must be a response simply for Oscar's sake.

Fear of Rejection or Abandonment

Fear of rejection or abandonment may have significant implications for treatment. There are several ways in which this fear can be realized. In some cases, a child's rejection by family of origin can create a fear of abandonment within the individual's adult couple relationship. In other cases, the fear of rejection is prompted by the history of the couple's relationship, particularly if there has been a pattern of being traumatically abandoned. Investigating the family of origin through the use of one of our focused genograms is one of the best ways to uncover a history of rejection or abandonment. The client's interpretation of what happened in the family will usually reveal whether he or she felt neglected, unwanted, abandoned, or physically or emotionally abandoned. The Intersystems approach structures therapy so that the therapist is able to obtain a fairly accurate view of the etiology of the fear, thus inspiring effective treatment.

Mack presented a tragic picture of feeling abandoned. The therapist had discovered that Mack believed that his wife would eventually leave him; thus, he did not want to form a close bond to her. The therapist questioned why Mack felt that his wife would reject or abandon him and discovered that, when Mack was 5, he was playing with his younger brother at the top of a set of stairs in their home. His brother accidentally fell down the stairs and almost died. His parents dealt with this problem by sending Mack to live with relatives without any explanation. Further, he parents only saw him occasionally. The lesson that Mack learned was that the ones who love you will inevitably reject you.

The therapist suggested some family-of-origin work with him. Mack discussed what had happened with his parents, who explained to him that they loved both of their children but felt that because Mack was bigger, he might accidentally push his brother down the stairs again. They admitted to overreacting to the situation by sending him away and explained that the cost of supporting him and making trips to see him were beyond their budget. Thus, they sent money to the relatives, but only visited when they had the money to do so. This knowledge changed Mack's view of his parents and he began to work through his feelings of abandonment with his parents and how he had carried that fear to his marriage.

Fear of Dependency

When a fear of dependency is present, the therapist may have a difficult time treating the clients. In a context in which each person is responsible for his or her piece of the problem, it may be difficult for each partner to "trust" the other to do his or her part in providing for the other partner's needs. After all, by the time couples come to therapy, there have been a series of disappointments regarding each other's ability to fulfill the other's need. The fear of dependency can be expressed sexually. In order for many sexual needs to be fulfilled, the partners must depend on each other to be sensitive, aware, and willing to meet the partner's needs.

Blake and Mary entered therapy for Mary's lack of sexual desire. The Intersystems assessment showed that Blake never initiated sex; his rationale was that Mary was never interested. However, this was not always the case, and Mary complained that Blake had never really initiated sex with her. He forced her into the role of being the initiator. Blake's mother had died at childbirth. The therapist wanted to know more about how his mother's death had affected him. Blake's father was wealthy and never remarried. He hired nannies to rear Blake. His father modeled his life after Hugh Hefner. At an early age he played a "game" with Blake where his father bent Blake's toes back until he cried and then told him if he cried he was weak and he would continue to bend his toes. His father would often repeat that life was tough and it was every man for himself. Blake was also told that women would be attracted to him if he was successful, which would enable him to use them as long as he wanted and then move on.

The therapist realized that Blake's behavior was actually counterdependent. He avoided being dependent on anyone and acted as if he could handle all of life's issues completely on his own. This meant he expected his wife to pursue him while he proved to himself that he could live without her emotionally and sexually. The therapist worked with Blake to get him to understand his fear of being dependent and how that fear had been instilled in him from an early age. As Blake started to understand this pattern, the therapist could then coach him on ways to identify and express his needs to his wife.

These short case studies are illustrative of the various fears of intimacy. We focused more on one partner in order to be brief. As systems thinkers, we need to remain attentive to the idea that both partners are about equally differentiated. In other words, each partner is at roughly the same level of mental health. Specifically, when one partner manifests a strong fear of intimacy, there is likely to be another fear in the partner that may not manifest overtly. Any experienced clinician has noted that when one spouse gets better, the other gets worse; in many of these cases, the overt sexual problem serves to mask the problem in the other. When the partner with the overt problem improves, the other partner's pathology manifests itself. A systems therapist should not wait for this to happen. Rather, he or she must understand the systemic and interlocking nature of the pathology, as well as conduct an assessment to attempt to uncover the issue in the nonidentified partner. If this attempt is unsuccessful, the problem in the nonidentified partner will most likely appear later in treatment.

7

Working With Particular Populations

Introduction

Sexual expression is a bodily activity and any changes in bodily function as the result of aging, trauma, or illness can impact sexual function. The treatment of sexual problems within such populations historically has been underemphasized in the field of sex therapy and sex research. However, in the last few years, medical research has begun to devote much more attention to these matters (Porst & Buvat, 2003). For several reasons, we believe that sex therapists will see an increasing number of cases with chronically ill, elderly, or differently abled clients. First, thanks to medical advances, people are living longer with chronic illnesses, particularly HIV, cancer, and diabetes. Second, the aging of the baby boomers results in an increased prevalence of couples over age 50 who are committed to remaining as sexually active as they were decades ago. Third, advocates for disabled individuals have been vocal in demanding that society view the disabled as sexual beings with a right to sexual pleasure, resulting in more willingness on the part of the disabled to seek help when they face sexual difficulties. Finally, as research continues to demonstrate the need for (Leiblum, 2008; Rosen, 2007) and effectiveness of (Heiman, 2002) sex therapy, physicians are gaining greater awareness about how helpful a referral to a sex therapist can be. Thus, it is essential that sex therapists have at least a basic understanding of these types of problems and the ways to treat clients with illnesses and disabilities from an Intersystems perspective.

This chapter explores the sexual issues unique to individuals who may have a physical disability, chronic illness, or physical changes associated with the natural aging process. It provides specific treatment strategies to counter the most commonly occurring situations. We discuss the three facets of the problem that must be understood in treatment planning:

- the medical aspects of the problem and how it affects sexual functioning;
- the client's perception of and beliefs about the problem and how it affects his or her sexuality as well as the partner's perceptions of the problem; and
- the individual's or couple's resiliency and ability to adapt to change.

Sexual Difficulties Among Chronically Ill Individuals

Every disease will impact sexual functioning in unique ways. This section briefly reviews sexual problems in individuals with various types of chronic illness. The body's neurological, cardiovascular, endocrine, and reproductive systems provide the physiological basis of sexual response. Therefore, damage or disease to any or all of these systems as well as the psychological stress of having a chronic illness can create conditions that result in or exacerbate an already existing sexual dysfunction.

Clients With Neurological Illness

Illnesses such as Parkinson's disease, multiple sclerosis, stroke, and other neurological disorders can affect the physiology involved in sexual functioning; loss of sexual desire through degradation of neurological functioning as well as through psychological distress can occur in those with neurological disorders (Kalayjian & Morrell, 2000). Dysaesthesia (impairment of sensitivity) in the genital area may result in diminished arousal, preventing erection or reducing genital orgasmic capacity (Hulter & Lundberg, 1995). However, other neurological conditions (such as cerebral palsy) may have no effect on sexual function.

If sexual problems exist in an individual with a neurological illness that cannot be directly tied to the disease, the sexual problem may be psychogenic, such as the result of stress from having a chronic illness. In some cases it can also result from a failure to adapt the sexual repertoire to changes in physical ability. Even when neurological disease does not cause a sexual dysfunction, motor system changes, such as tremors, rigidity, and spasms can make certain sexual acts more awkward and potentially painful. Anticipatory anxiety in such situations can fuel the loss of desire, creating a self-fulfilling belief that spirals into further sexual difficulty. By adapting the sexual repertoire to fit the limitations of the disease, the couple can successfully re-establish a working sexual relationship. Clinicians should review strategies here and in Chapter 5 that detail appropriate interventions for reducing anxiety.

Clients With Cardiovascular Illness

Træen and Olsen (2007) found the prevalence of sexual problems for people with heart disease to be about double that in the general population. In the age group 40–49 years, 73% of men with heart disease experienced a sexual difficulty, typically erectile dysfunction (ED). However, psychological factors (including resiliency and the ability to cope with a life-threatening illness) were found to be more important than medical and other factors in determining the prevalence of sexual problems in this particular population. Additionally, medical or sexual myths and fears may adversely affect a client's sexual function. For example, a male client suffered a minor heart attack. Although the doctors told him having sex was not risky, he avoided sex for several years because of his fear of precipitating another heart attack. His sexual mythology was that the stress of sex might kill him.

Oncology Clients

Cancer and its treatment can impact every aspect of the sexual response cycle, with estimates of sexual dysfunction in this particular population ranging from 40 to 100% (Derogatis & Kourlesis, 1981). Loss of interest in sex upon diagnosis and during treatment of cancer can readily be expected and may result from worry, depression, nausea, pain, or fatigue, as well the physiological side effects of treatment. Anxiety and preoccupation with cancer and possible death may distract from sexual desire and the ability to stay focused on pleasure during sexual activity.

The most common problems associated with cancer are loss of sexual desire, ED in men, and dyspareunia in women. Sexual pain disorders in the genital area can occur after chemotherapy, radiation therapy, or hormonal treatment. Each of these treatments produces slightly different side effects regarding pain, so clinicians should ask a variety of questions about the specific nature of the pain that is being experienced. Other cancer-related problems may be difficulty in arousal and lubrication and changes in genital sensation for women. For men, retrograde ejaculation (anejacu-lation) is a less frequent but still distressing side effect of some treatments. Although this section reviews the aftereffects of surgery, chemotherapy, radiation, and hormonal treatment, it is also important to note that medi-cations used to treat the pain of cancer and its treatment can also produce sexual dysfunction; this is discussed in a later section of this chapter.

Depending on the type of cancer, surgery can sever or damage impor-tant nerves, reducing sensation as well as erectile ability for men and lubri-cating capacity for women. For women, healing from pelvic or genital surgery can cause scar tissue, reducing the size and shape of the vagina and resulting in dyspareunia. Pelvic or genital surgery that results in the loss of reproductive organs often has a psychological impact, with indi-viduals questioning their gendered and sexual selves.

Prostate cancer is a particularly distressing type of cancer for men because of the real possibility of loss of sexual functioning or life. To those who face this, it is a difficult trade-off; we have treated men who have said they would rather die than lose their sexual capacity. Although newer, "nerve-sparing" surgical procedures may result in greater restoration of erectile capacity, it is estimated that 10–40% of men who have had a radi-cal prostatectomy regain fully functional erections (Smith et al., 2000). In our practice, men who undergo the nerve-sparing procedure often return to normal functioning, but only after a significant period of time. During this period of time, they wonder if they have lost the ability to have an erection permanently. They need to be reassured that normal functioning or nearly normal functioning will return, but they need to be patient and find other means of sexual expression until that time. Additionally, the use of PDE-5 inhibitors has been shown to be effective with the majority of postoperative men (Brock et al., 2003).

Likewise, women may feel less feminine after breast or genital surgery. A hysterectomy or clitorectomy may negatively impact ability to achieve orgasm. Women often fear that their partners may be turned off by the scarring and loss of breasts or outer genitals and may question their sexual desirability as their body image is negatively impacted from the operation.

Radiation is another treatment modality that can produce fatigue, nau-sea, diarrhea, and other conditions that reduce sexual desire. If the tis-sue targeted includes the genitalia, inflammation and irritation may make sexual activity painful. Pelvic radiation may also change the shape and mucosal layer of the vagina, leading to dyspareunia. Irritation of the pros-tate gland or urethra from radiation, as well as scar tissue after healing from treatment, can cause painful ejaculation or ED.

Chemotherapy is another important treatment for cancer. Women undergoing chemotherapy may often have symptoms of early menopause and may have an increase in sexual pain or yeast infections as a result of the radiation drying and thinning the vaginal lining. In men, chemotherapy can interfere with ejaculation of semen, which can result in the perception of a weaker or drier orgasm. Individuals receiving chemotherapy often experience decreased sexual desire because hair loss, weight fluctuation, and the presence of a long-term serious illness negatively impact sexual self-image.

Hormone therapy, such as tamoxifen (which prevents the abnormal use or production of estrogen, progestin, or testosterone), may also result in diminished desire and arousal for both men and women. For men, treatments for prostate cancer that involve reducing the testosterone level as low as possible frequently reduce desire and arousal.

The clinician will need to research the type of treatment used for each type of cancer in order to develop a more complete picture of the predictable side effects. Once the side effects are understood, the issue becomes that of helping the individual and the couple deal with the short-term effects and learn how to live with the long-term impact of the illness.

Clients With Diabetes

Diabetes is a chronic illness that impacts the neurological, cardiovascular, and endocrinological systems of an individual, frequently having an adverse impact on sexual functioning. As diabetes narrows blood vessels, nerves are damaged, resulting in problems with circulation and organ function. Hypoactive sexual desire may exist in individuals with diabetes because a general loss of energy diminishes sex drive and the loss of bladder control from nerve damage negatively impacts one's sense of sexual attractiveness. For men, the impact of diabetes on sexual function is direct and significant; between 35 and 75% of males with diabetes experience some loss of erectile functioning (Spector, Leiblum, Carey, & Rosen, 1993).

In women, problems with sexual functioning, beyond the problems mentioned previously, have not been clearly established, but some research has shown that diabetic women have greater chances of arousal problems for some of the same reasons men do—predominately a lack of lubrication. Some diabetic women may experience more difficulty reaching orgasm than women without diabetes. Other studies have linked diabetic women and desire disorders, although this may be an artifact of poor self-image and the stress and depression associated with having an illness (Rockliffe-Fidler & Keimle, 2003). Additionally, physical complications of diabetes, such as the greater occurrence of genitourinary infections (GUIs), may also impact diabetic women's sexual functioning by increasing chances for sexual pain or discomfort and reducing the desire to engage in sexual acts.

Frequently, diabetes is diagnosed as a consequence of seeking help for a sexual problem, usually men experiencing ED, which is often the first warning sign of diabetes. Rosen (2007) notes that uncontrolled diabetes leading to nerve damage may also contribute to retrograde ejaculation. Uncontrolled diabetes also leads to a reduction in testosterone, which may present as diminished desire. The importance of conducting a thorough Intersystems assessment (individual-biological aspect of the problem) for all sexual problems is underscored by the fact that many men who present for ED treatment may not have had the requisite medical screening or testing. Without a screening, the therapist cannot rule out diabetes as a factor in the etiology of a client's sexual problems. Asking basic questions about a family history of diabetes, recent changes in levels of thirst and need to urinate, blurred vision, or numbness in the limbs is important. Positive answers to these questions demand a referral for a thorough medical evaluation for diabetes.

Finally, several psychosocial factors have been identified as contributing to sexual dysfunctions in populations with chronic illness, including relationship dissatisfaction (Plaud et al., 1996), depressed mood (Seidman & Roose, 2000), and body image concerns (Schiavi, Stimmel, Mandeli, Schreiner-Engel, & Ghizzani, 1995).

Sexual Difficulties Among Physically Disabled Individuals

Special consideration must be placed on understanding the nature and etiology of a client with a disability or physical limitation. The effect of the disability may be a mix of psychological reactions and having to deal with physical limitations. Individuals with a lifelong disability, such as spina bifida, may have issues different from those who face a recent or adult-onset disabling event, such as a spinal cord injury (SCI). Those with a lifelong disability may have experienced a lack of sex education and socialization during adolescence, resulting in sexual dysfunctions that center on anxiety, the lack of interpersonal skills, or lack of exposure to potential partners and formative sexual experiences. Such anxiety, lack of early experiences, etc. can impact the current sexual relationship by reducing sexual communication and feelings of sexual competence, impairing sexual performance, and inhibiting the desire to form intimate relationships. Clients who have a physical disability from a recent or adult-onset disabling event may carry issues such as grief, impaired sexual functioning, and a disrupted sexual self-image. Therefore, learning ways to find sexual pleasure that go beyond what might be considered typical sexual behavior and adopting an image of oneself as a person who can be sexually desired and can show a desire for others is necessary (Tepper, 1997).

Spinal cord injuries frequently result in changes in sexual arousability; for men, they change erectile function and, for women, lubrication. However, the likelihood of whether one will lose all genital sexual function depends on the location of the injury and its severity. Specifically, those who sustain injuries that are higher up on the spine and that are less severe are more likely to regain functioning than those with lower and more severe injuries (Soler, Previnaire, Denys, & Chartier-Kastler, 2007). Despite where the injury occurs, a lack or diminishment of desire is typical (Whipple & Komisaruk, 2002; Tepper, 1997) and is associated with psychological problems such as depression and maladaptive coping mechanisms.

For some, sexual problems may result from their response to societal views of disabled individuals as unappealing or asexual. This view can become internalized so that the person believes the societal view is correct. Internalization of these negative attitudes tends to exacerbate any physical limitations in sexual functioning (Tepper, 2000). It is essential that therapists assess a client's self-image and understanding of his or her sexual problem. According to Gill and Hough (2007), women with a disability report that feeling attractive and desirable is more important to their sexual well-being than their genital functioning. If an individual with a disability does not feel attractive or desirable, such feelings can reduce the instances in which the disabled partner initiates sex or responds to a partner's invitations. Consequently, a negative self-image diminishes opportunities for intimate relationships and sexual activity, which in turn reinforces the client's belief that he or she is undesirable.

The therapist must help disabled persons see themselves in a positive light. They must know that they can be valued and desired in a relationship, have a right to their own sexual pleasure, and—no matter what physical limitations they have—can give pleasure to another. In short, a person with a disability is not sexually disabled and the therapist's job may be to turn this easily made statement into the client's fully embraced belief and practice.

Sexual Difficulties Among Geriatric Individuals and Couples

Sexual dysfunction in the elderly can signal either mental or physical disease (Laumann et al., 2005) or be a response to sociocultural conditions that stigmatize sexuality in older people (Camacho & Reyes-Ortiz, 2005). Physical changes associated with aging may produce sexual difficulties and a main contributor to age-related sexual dysfunction is poor health, including heart disease, high blood pressure, or diabetes, as well as the treatment of these health problems. The earlier discussion of sexual difficulties among those with chronic illness should be reviewed as applicable to geriatric clients in poor physical health. Additionally, many elderly clients may be on multiple medications that may impact sexual function. Although Table 7.1 lists medications that may impact sexual function, clinicians may need to consult *Sexual Pharmacology* (Seagraves & Balon, 2003; Crenshaw & Goldberg, 1996) for information that is more detailed. Because some clients may not recall all of their medications or dosages, we recommend that therapists mail medical history forms to the clients to complete at home where they have access to their prescription information.

Physiologically, as men get older, they may experience a host of sexual changes, including a decreased ability to have:

- spontaneous erection;
- increased need for foreplay;
- decreased penile sensitivity;
- decreased premature ejaculation;
- increased retarded ejaculation;
- increased length of refractory period;
- increased episodes of losing erection without orgasm; and
- increased likelihood of loss of erection.

ED is so common that it is almost normative; 52% of men between ages 40 and 70 having experienced some degree of erectile difficulty (Derby, Araujo, Johannes, Feldman, & McKinlay, 2000).

The major issue facing older women is the impact of menopause on sexuality. Some researchers (see, for example, Dennerstein, 1996; Riley, 1991) have shown that the biological changes associated with menopause can result in arousal difficulties and sexual pain. The loss of estrogen during menopause can trigger hot flashes and vaginal atrophy, making arousal physiologically more difficult. Additionally, low androgen levels

TABLE 7.1 Drugs That May Adversely Affect Sexual Function

Class	Drug
CNS acting	Antidepressants (including tricyclics and SSRIs)
	Antipsychotics
	Tranquilizers
	Anorexiants
Cardiovascular	Digoxin
	Older antihypertensives (reserpine, guanethidine, hydralazine)
	β-Blockers (especially propranolol, metoprolol, penbutolol, pindolol, timolol)
	Certain α-blockers (clonidine, guanfacine, prazosin) and l-blockers (labetalol)
	Methyldopa
	Thiazide diuretics
	Spironolactone
	Calcium channel blockers (fairly low risk)
Allergy related	Corticosteroids
	Theophylline
	Bronchodilators
Antifungals	Fluconazole
	Ketoconazole
	Itraconazole
Recreational	Marijuana
	Alcohol
Nonprescription	Antihistamines (chlorpheniramine, diphenhydramine, chlotrimeton)
	Decongestants
	Cimetidine

in women may decrease sexual desire and pleasure. However, some of our clients have noted that menopause gives them a more carefree approach to sex, enhancing their enjoyment and satisfaction as the risk of unwanted pregnancy ends.

A review of current health status and medical history should highlight the organic basis of sexual difficulties and indicate the client's general capacity to engage in sexual activities. When cardiovascular health or cognitive ability (such as in cases of dementia) is in question, clinicians should advise clients to get a physician's consent before conducting sex therapy. After attending to the medical aspects of aging (such as illness and medications), clinicians need to assess how clients view their age and sexuality. Psychological factors, including the quality of sexual relationships, sexual attitudes, and measures of well-being, are frequently better prognostic factors of sexual dysfunction than physiological measures (Cawood & Bancroft, 1996; Dennerstein, Dudley, Hopper, & Burger, 1997). What this means is that older couples are perfectly capable of sharing sexual pleasure in spite of illness and medications so long as they have a positive view of themselves sexually.

Depression and anxiety have been associated with the likelihood of erectile and lubrication difficulties in older men and women (Laumann et al., 2005). Thus, the clinician must closely examine the degree of depression in this population. Among women and men over age 40, relationship factors were found to have a significant impact on the prevalence of one or more sexual problems (Laumann et al., 2005). In one study, a low level of relationship satisfaction increased the likelihood of anorgasmia among women. However, for men, being in an uncommitted relationship was positively associated with erectile difficulties. It may be that the men were sexually anxious when with a new partner or in a relationship where, in their minds, commitment might depend on being able to perform sexually.

Another important issue for elderly individuals is partner availability, and a great deal of research has determined that there is a "use it or lose it" phenomenon where infrequent sexual activity increases the likelihood of erectile and lubrication difficulties. Elderly singles living in residential care facilities are most at risk because of their extremely limited ability to meet new partners and engage in sexual behaviors in front of staff members who typically discourage such expression (Gott, 2004; 2006). Further, society tends to view the elderly as sexually "dead," so assessment should include the clients' internalization of social messages or their ability to challenge stereotypes successfully. Conflicts between their own sexual values and the sexual norms of the dominant culture may result in sexual difficulties. Social norms that do not permit the elderly to share affection or present themselves as sexual beings can have a negative impact on sexual function and overall relationship satisfaction.

An elderly partner's poor health status may contribute to a sexual difficulty in the relationship. The stress of acting as caretaker for one's partner may negatively impact sexual desire due to fatigue, worry, anxiety, and perhaps even resentment toward the partner. We believe that when partners can show that they care for one another intimately and are able to express their affection and sexual desires openly, there is a lowered risk of developing more complex sexual issues (see, for example, Weeks, Gambescia, & Jenkins, 2003).

Treatment Strategies for Special Populations

In treating the sexual problems of individuals with age-related physiologi-cal decline, a disability, or chronic illness, attending to the way illness, disability, or the aging process impacts an individual's sense of self and sexuality may be even more important for the sex therapist than treating the particular impact on physiological function. This task would involve utilizing the individual's and couple's intrinsic flexibility and coping mechanisms to foster a healthy sexuality and expanding the definition of what constitutes "sex," as necessary to adapt successfully to the client's particular physical reality (Sipski & Alexander, 1997). Any treatment plan with individuals in these particular populations should probably include:

- coordinating treatment with physicians;
- providing psychoeducation to reduce modifiable risk factors;
- learning to compensate for the consequences of the illness or disability;
- grief work, expanding the definition of sexuality;
- creating a new self-image as a sexual being; and
- relational therapy to address the impact of the disability or illness on the relationship.

Collaborate With Client's Physicians

With nearly all of the particular populations under consideration in this chapter, it is important to keep open the lines of communication with the client's primary care physicians, oncologists, endocrinologists, and pain management doctors. The therapist's goals in working with the client's physician is to understand the unique nature of the client's illness or dis-ability and its impact on sexual functioning, how the physician's current treatment strategies connect with or contraindicate sex therapy, and the physician's prognosis, so as to better assess the client's goals for sex ther-apy. In situations where consultations with physicians are not possible, the relevant resources provided in Table 7.2 offer a general understanding of the issues facing the client.

To coordinate with physicians, it will be necessary to obtain permis-sion for the physician to release medical information. Clinicians are advised to use standardized forms that detail the types of information to be exchanged, the reasons for or uses of the information, and a date at which the release becomes void. Working with the client's physician lets

TABLE 7.2   Internet Resources

Web site	Web address
American Cancer Society—sexuality for men and their partners	http://www.cancer.org/docroot/MIT/MIT_7_1x_SexualityforMenandTheirPartners.asp
American Cancer Society—sexuality for women and their partners	http://www.cancer.org/docroot/MIT/MIT_7_1x_SexualityforWomenandTheirPartners
Sexual activity and heart disease or stroke	http://216.185.112.5/presenter.jhtml?identifier=4714 asp
Sexual dysfunction in women: What can I do if sex isn't working for me?	http://familydoctor.org/612.xml
Age page: sexuality in later life	http://www.niapublications.org/engagepages/sexuality.asp
Why safe sex is a menopause priority	http://www.regardinghealth.com/nam/RHO/2004/06/Article.aspx?bmkEMC=14610
Sex after 50: how to hold onto the passion	http://www.mayoclinic.com/health/sexual-health/HA00035
AARP study: sexuality at midlife and beyond: 2004 update of attitudes and behaviors—women beyond 50	http://www.aarp.org/research/family/lifestyles/2004_sexuality.html
The National Multiple Sclerosis Society	http://www.nationalmssociety.org
Sexual Health Network	http://www.sexualhealth.com

the client know that the therapist is serious about getting all the information needed to help the client. Even the treatment of ED via medical approaches in the general population results in better outcomes when sex therapists work collaboratively with physicians to help clients re-engage sexually. Some clients are unaware that they are experiencing sexual side effects from drugs. Therapists may need to collaborate with the client's physicians in order to change pharmaceutical treatments in a way that may minimize the negative sexual effects.

Physicians are sometimes not aware that their patient is having a sexual difficulty because clients are embarrassed to tell the doctor. At a minimum, the physician and/or therapist should counsel clients about timing sexual activity with prescription use, especially medications that may blunt desire or interfere with performance. It will be important to understand how the client experiences the medication (drowsiness, loss of focus, etc.) and strategize ways to work within the constraints of its effects. In addition to drugs prescribed to treat any physical ailments, clinicians should take into account any psychotropic medications used to manage concomitant depression or anxiety. Selective serotonin reuptake inhibitors (SSRIs), such as Lexapro, Paxil, and Zoloft, are frequently prescribed for depression and may worsen desire and arousal problems. See Table 7.1 for a brief list of commonly prescribed drugs that affect sexual functioning.

Lastly, therapists may need to work with physicians when sexual difficulties can be treated medically. With many men in the populations under consideration here, oral medications such as Viagra (sildenafil) and Caverject (an injectible system using the drug apomorphine) can be used to increase erectile potential significantly. PDE-5 inhibitors (Viagra, for example) can often be successfully prescribed to diabetic men with ED (Carson, 2002). However, studies show that medical interventions work best when combined with psychotherapy (see McCarthy & Fucito, 2005; Rosen, 2007)—reflecting the fact that ED often has a psychological overlay, so both the physical and psychological must be treated concurrently. Currently, there are no pharmaceutical interventions to restore women's sexual arousal or orgasmic capacity. Any such use of pharmaceuticals for women is considered "off label" and must be addressed in terms of interaction effects with other prescribed medications. In our experience, the effect of PDE-5, testosterone, and other pharmaceuticals in women is very mixed and not currently recommended for sexual dysfunctions.

Provide Psychoeducation

Frequently, sex therapy with the particular populations discussed earlier involves psychoeducation and providing pragmatic responses to changes in physical functioning. Basic psychoeducation can help address modifiable risk factors such as smoking, alcohol consumption, lack of exercise, and poor eating habits that diminish sexual behavior. Therapists should counsel clients on how to reduce their risks of becoming overly fatigued through stress management and achieving a balance in work and leisure life. They can also obtain pamphlets on diet, exercise, and risk reduction specifically for diabetics through the American Diabetes Association website: http://professional.diabetes.org/Default.aspx. The role of the therapist in this intervention is to make clear the links between lifestyle and sexual function as well as help the client establish and work toward health habits that promote good sexual functioning.

Clients who leak urine or fecal matter during sex may be very embarrassed and avoid sex. Loss of bladder control can be compensated for by educating clients on the need to void the bladder and limit the intake of liquids prior to sexual activity. Enhancement of bladder control can be achieved for women through Kegel exercises (see Bley, 2007a). Besides developing some practical solutions, we have noted that some men in our practices are actually turned on by the loss of urine and tell their partners, who in turn discount this as "just being nice."

For clients experiencing arousal difficulties, therapists should instruct them on the use of an appropriate lubricant. Unflavored silicone or water-based lubricants are best because flavored versions typically have glycerin or some other type of sweetener that may exacerbate a yeast infection in individuals with diabetes or whose immune systems have been compromised. Further, it is important that individuals with neural damage do not use stimulating lubricants or those that provide heat on contact. Such lubricants can irritate or chemically burn the genital area, especially vulval tissue. This might create a wound that, due to diminished sensitivity, may not be recognized until an infection has developed.

Therapists should review a variety of touches and positions to reduce physical discomfort or sexual pain, instruct clients on the use lubricants and dilators, and encourage the practice of relaxation techniques. Using pillows, bolsters, or cushions can minimize injury from surgery wounds or spastic limbs. They may also be useful for clients who have chronic back pain and need to avoid too much stress on certain parts of their spine. For those clients with colostomy bags, the therapist should advise them to drain bags and reduce fluid intake in advance of sexual activity. The nonprofit organization Disability Resources offers links on its Web site to decorative covers for bags, which often can be rolled or folded away. If appropriate, couples should be encouraged to incorporate an individual's prosthetic devices into their lovemaking, reinforcing the idea that the artificial limb does not detract from the client's sexuality; rather, it is, in fact, what makes him or her unique and lovable. Further information on practical skills counseling can be found in the works of Mitchell Tepper and the resources listed in Table 7.3.

TABLE 7.3   Bibliotherapy and Psychoeducation

Source	Authors or editors
The Illustrated Guide to Better Sex for People With Chronic Pain	Robert W. Rothrock, PA-C, and Gabriella D'Amore, PA-C
MS and Intimacy: Managing Specific Issues	Tanya Radford
Sexual Concerns When Illness or Disability Strikes	Carol L. Sandowski, MSW, ACSW
The Sexual Politics of Disability: Untold Desires	Tom Shakespeare, Dominic Davies, Kath Gillespie-Sells, editors
Sexuality After Spinal Cord Injury: Answers to Your Questions	Stanley H. Ducharme and Kathleen M. Gill
Sexuality and Spinal Cord Injury	Sylvia Eichner McDonald, Willa M. Lloyd, Donna Murphy, and Margaret Gretchen Russert
Choices: A Guide to Sex Counseling with Physically Disabled Adults	Maureen E. Neistadt, MS, OTR/L, and Maureen Freda, OTR/L
Providing Comprehensive Sexual Health Care in Spinal Cord Injury Rehabilitation: Continuing Education and Training for Health Care Professionals	Mitchell S. Tepper
Sexual Function in People With Disability and Chronic Illness: A Health Professional's Guide	Marca L. Sipski and Craig J. Alexander
Sexuality and Chronic Illness: A Comprehensive Approach	Leslie R. Schover, PhD, and Søren Buus Jensen, MD

Address Anxiety, Misinformation, and Myths

Often, individuals with a disability or chronic illness are anxious about engaging in sexual activity. This anxiety is combined with stress from the illness and can result in performance anxiety and exacerbate the previously existing sexual problems. Instructing clients on thought-stopping and other anxiety reduction techniques found in Chapter 5 of this book are appropriate. Discussing the illness or disability openly in session may be the only place where the couple communicates about their real sexual limitations and their stress and anxiety about sex.

Connected with anxiety surrounding sexual activity may be a host of myths, such as that any sexual acts could be fatal or make the illness worse. Faulty beliefs and a lack of practical knowledge about sex and illness or disability also get in the way of healthy sexuality. Researchers found that a large percentage of those over 50 lacked information regarding arousal in aging women, the role of hormones in male impotence, the ability of women to be satisfied sexually without intercourse, and the ability of a couple to have a satisfying sexual relationship without intercourse (Adams et al., 1996). Individuals may have basic sex information; however, therapists would be wise to dispel myths and assess the accuracy of the clients' beliefs about sexuality and ability, illness, and aging. The therapist must listen carefully for sexual misinformation, elicit information about what is pertinent to their situation, and give corrective information.

The clients' cognitions, beliefs, self-images, the illness/ability or aging issue, and their relationship may be useful to know. The therapist should ask partners to list the maladaptive beliefs they have about their sexuality and their physical situation and then help them to change those beliefs by (1) pointing out distortions in their cognitive processes, and (2) correcting inaccurate information about sexuality or their physical circumstances. The therapist may need to explore these beliefs from a psychodynamic perspective if they are core beliefs or otherwise related to other core aspects of the person's self-identity. This exploration could involve an examination of psychosexual development and how these early life experiences are continually functioning in the background of awareness. These very early experiences may still be affecting how partners interpret and respond to their current situation. In many cases, clients have adopted ideas about what it is like to be chronically ill and disabled from watching other members of their family struggle with illness. Sometimes what clients have learned about how people who are disabled or ill manage their sex lives is based on the implicit and/or explicit messages they receive from other family members, friends, or the media.

As we suggested earlier, aging, illness, or disability may have changed the client's levels of desire. Level of desire, especially a discrepancy in desire, should be closely examined and an attempt made to reconcile differences in a couple. In order to address this, the therapist will need to explore the impact of the illness on the couple dynamics. For example, one partner may become the caretaker for the other, thus creating a parent–child relationship, as it is sometimes called. This type of relational dynamic is part of a much larger dynamic that affects more than the sexual relationship. It could be understood that desire and activity are two different phenomena. One partner may please the other sensually or sexually without having sexual desire just because he or she wants to give the other a gift.

Attend to Affect and Self-Image

Depression, anxiety, guilt, anger, and denial may all be expected reactions to a sudden onset of disability or news of a chronic illness. When this occurs, it may be necessary to determine whether grief counseling is necessary prior to beginning sex therapy. For clients with early onset disability, grief work may focus on the denial of opportunities that other nondisabled individuals have had in their lives. For clients with sudden-onset loss of limbs or mobility or chronic illness, the grief work may need to focus on coming to terms with their new bodies and their physical limitations. In both cases, it is important to restore or create in the client a positive sexual self-image.

The development of a positive sexual self-image can come through cognitive and experiential interventions, in both individual and relational therapies. For those in a relationship, the change of self-image should be processed in both individual and conjoint sessions. In the case of loss of limb, for example, the therapist might acknowledge the prosthetic leg and follow up with questions like:

- What have you done to mourn the loss of your leg? What have you done to welcome your new limb? (Here clinicians may want to consider having rituals to let go of the missing limb as well as to embrace the new one.)
- How has losing a limb changed how others view you? How has it changed how you view yourself?
- How do you feel about yourself as a man or woman with a "bionic" limb and how does your partner feel about it?
- Once the development of a realistic self-image has begun, move quickly to developing a positive sexual self-image through questions such as: How has the prosthetic device changed your sexual behavior? How can we improve things, such as trying different positions, pillows, and other devices that might give you support?

A negative self-image may lead clients to avoid any type of sexual relationship. Therapy for them will initially need to address the development of a positive self-image as outlined earlier, with the encouragement to begin experimenting with relationships as soon as possible. We reduce reluctance to date by letting them know that it is only casual dating to gain experience and even advise them not to get interested personally, but rather to begin by treating the dating as "an experiment." Some individuals may have developed a virtually phobic avoidance of trying to develop a relationship. The therapist will need to process their avoidance feelings again and again. This process will surface their negative beliefs about their sexuality and value in a relationship.

Expanding the Sexual Repertoire

An emphasis may need to be placed on expanding the repertoire of pleasurable activities—exploring new positions, techniques, and devices or sexual aids when dealing with individuals with disability or illness. This expansion of the sexual repertoire may need to be conducted in conjunction with psychoeducation to dispel myths and cognitive work to reduce the exclusive focus on intercourse and coital orgasm as the only "real" way to have sex.

In expanding the sexual repertoire, it is important for therapists to focus on pleasure over performance. Most clients think that good sex is about a particular type of performance made impossible by their illness or disability. The goal of sex is to give and receive sexual and sensual pleasure, whatever the performance and outcome happen to be. Once clients accept this as the goal of sex, anxiety will be reduced and the therapist can then help them determine the most effective ways for them to obtain the pleasurable sensations they desire.

Typically, expanding what is sexually pleasurable involves giving permission, bibliotherapy, and some sensate focus. In assigning reading or viewing materials in the bibliotherapy portion, therapists should take the clients' age, religiosity, degree of conventionality, and educational level into account. We frequently suggest Alex Comfort's books (see Chapter 11), but know that this may not appeal to or be appropriate for all our clients. One strategy we use to tailor bibliotherapy to particular clients is to have them search Amazon.com using the term "sex positions" and then scan the reviewer's comments about the nature of the book. For couples needing to alter their position, many books are available, but different books have different appeal to different clients.

It is important to encourage in clients a sense of trial and error and that the pursuit of pleasurable activities is an adventure for both of them. Couples who are looking for easy answers or for the therapist simply to tell them what to do will be disappointed. Beginning with a sense of adventure and being given permission to be creative help to inspire them to find their own solutions.

Enhance Couple Communication

The onset of illness, disability, or age-related decline may significantly influence couple dynamics, producing impaired communication, unwelcome role changes and role strain, and challenges adapting to the new situation. Partners may have difficulty communicating their sexual needs and desires to each other and may feel guilt about having sexual feelings toward someone who is ill or in pain from a disability. These are issues that couples may be very reluctant to discuss. The therapist can gently encourage them to bring these issues out. Sometimes it may be necessary to meet with each partner individually to get a sense of what each is actually thinking and then decide how to bring their concerns into the couple session.

One strategy that frequently works in getting couples to communicate about their sexual needs is sensate focus. Such an intervention allows the therapist to encourage some type of sensual activity and at the same time facilitate communication. This exercise will also reveal underlying obstacles to the couple having better sexual expression. Additionally, accessing the client's sense of humor, fun, and creativity will afford the client a sense of empowerment and also keep the perspective on sexual enjoyment, not dysfunction.

Address the Self of the Therapist

As noted earlier, practical education can be provided on how to deal with involuntary elimination, medication side effects, and "limb management" in individuals with spastic or artificial limbs or paralysis. However, before providing any information to clients, therapists may need to educate themselves in greater detail than provided here about the client's particular illness or disability. It is essential that clinicians provide accurate information in an easygoing, matter-of-fact way. Therapists should deal openly and directly with the individual's illness, abilities, and needs because avoiding subjects may imply negative judgment and will adversely affect the therapeutic alliance.

Sex for individuals with disabilities or who are older is too frequently viewed as an invisible problem complicating or contraindicating the initiation of any intrapsychic or interpersonal therapy (Pangman & Seguire, 2000). As such, clients may not have ever been asked directly about their levels of sexual interest and activity, and desire to improve their sexual lives. Many of those in these groups may have given up hope that anyone cares or that any help is possible. Therapists need to understand how their own age, health, and physical ability may be "read" by clients. Older clients may be reluctant to tell a therapist who is the same age as their child or grandchild about their sexual problems. Individuals with a disability may be highly sensitive to a perceived lack of empathy from therapists without a disability. Thus, being active in challenging stereotypes and firmly believing in the client's right to sexual pleasure and ability to have a satisfying sexual and intimate relationship becomes an important first step that therapists should take well before they even see their clients.

Therapists may experience multiple countertransference issues with this population and may fall prey to the cultural stereotype that chronically ill individuals, older couples, or individuals with disabilities are not sexually interested or active. Therapists may also have fears of their own illness, disability, and death. The idea that they may someday be like the people they are treating may arouse so much fear and anxiety that they block any discussion that gets to the depth of the client's current despair and hopelessness. Therapists must be open to their own vulnerability if they are to help those in such a vulnerable position. If therapists begin to focus on their own fears or beliefs in sessions and have difficulty getting to the client's painful emotions or avoiding subjects, it is essential that they seek supervision, possibly referring the clients to a more appropriate therapist. Chapter 8 addresses this issue in greater detail.

Section II

Practice Issues and
Resources for Sex Therapy

8

Practice and Ethical Issues

Introduction

In addition to the professional practice and ethical issues that apply to traditional psychotherapy, sex therapists have special considerations, primarily because of the nature of the topic in the field in which they work. This chapter outlines the considerations that need to be made during treatment, the scope of practice and referrals, ethical issues, and gaining an awareness of the therapist's values and biases as he or she provides treatment.

The Process and Structure of Treatment

Client Identification

Beginning sex therapists need to consider several issues throughout the process of treatment, including client identification, problem definition, and goal setting (Brown & Sollod, 1988). Client identification can be particularly complicated in sex therapy cases for several reasons. First, the couple coming to seek treatment is composed of two individuals, who independently have varying agendas from the other and may try to build an alliance with the therapist and implement their agenda. For example, one couple came to treatment to address hypoactive sexual desire disorder on the part of the wife. During the assessment, it became clear that her lack of desire was complicated by several factors, including physiological limitations (a back injury that compromised her ability to feel sensations), difficulty in being able to communicate her needs to her partner without feeling blamed, and depression. Her hope was that therapy would "convince" her partner that he bore some responsibility in the sexual problems they were having, most notably related to his blameful attitude toward her and the disruption in their communication. His agenda in treatment was to "get help for her," not acknowledging any responsibility for his part in the treatment process. In this way, the husband viewed the sex therapy process as one by which he would function as a co-therapist in order to be of assistance to his partner rather than as a full participant in treatment.

Although Masters and Johnson utilized the nonsymptomatic partner in sex therapy as an informant and therapeutic surrogate (1970), the difference in perspectives of who is the identified client has significant implications for goal setting, intervention development and implementation, and, ultimately, treatment compliance (Brown & Sollod, 1988). Clients may agree in session to treatment goals proposed by the therapist, but secretly disagree with the goals of treatment. For example, in the case described previously, if the therapist outlines treatment goals that engender both partners to be active partners in the treatment process, the therapist may be viewed by the husband as siding with the wife's agenda, thereby ignoring his needs. The end result may be a premature drop-out in treatment or sabotaging interventions. For this reason, it is crucial that the therapist address the question of client identification early in the treatment process to avoid later complications in treatment. The therapist may need to reframe the problem carefully in a way that includes the needs of both partners. Therapy should not proceed beyond this point until the partners agree on their problem and goal of treatment.

Second, what is in the best interest of the couple's relationship may contradict one or both agendas of the individuals within the couple (Hill & Coll, 1992). In the preceding case example, it seemed clear that each partner wanted to put the responsibility of the problem on the other partner. Blaming the other partner, however, is not likely to resolve the problem between the two. In this way, the therapist's agenda (preservation of the couple relationship) may be different from each individual's agenda. If the therapist's agenda takes precedence over the couple's agenda, the couple may feel as if their concerns are not adequately heard by the therapist, thus compromising a couple's involvement in the treatment process.

Problem Definition

In many sex therapy cases, clients and therapists can have difficulty clarifying the problem to be solved. According to the Intersystems approach

(Weeks, 1994), multiple factors can contribute to the development and maintenance of a sexual problem between two individuals. Such factors include individual biological factors, individual psychological factors, dyadic/relational factors, family-of-origin factors, and sociocultural factors. The definition of the problem can expand from the sexual symptomology to that of the couple's communication patterns, an individual's physical diagnoses, or the messages received from one's family of origin related to sexuality, etc. The conceptualization of the problem in a certain manner ultimately guides treatment goals and interventions.

Further, the labeling of the problem as a "dysfunction" may be counterproductive to treatment (Brown & Sollod, 1988). When couples come to treatment with a sexual concern, they may already be ashamed, feel that they are not "normal," and be using all of the strengths they have to get through the door of a sex therapist's office. To classify sexual behavior (even behavior not within the scope of the presenting problem) as "deviant" or "abnormal" based on the therapist's value system will only increase the client's anxiety and reduce the likelihood of treatment effectiveness. The therapist needs to be cautious that the stance reflected to clients about their issues follows contemporary professional standards rather than those of the therapist's beliefs and attitudes.

Goal Setting

Goal setting in sex therapy is an ethical issue because the direction of treatment can be dictated by the therapist's values, the values of the couple, and society's views and perspectives on a given problem. Which perspective takes priority and why? Inherent in the therapist–client relationship is the element of a therapist's power. Regardless of the therapeutic stance or the therapist's intention, the therapist may be observed by the client to be in a place of greater power. The therapist needs to be mindful of the values he or she is imposing on the treatment process, particularly related to the development and implementation of goals. Therapists may find themselves advocating a certain position, set of attitudes, or values and in fact be creating greater difficulty for clients from varying cultural or religious backgrounds (Bancroft, 1981).

Another ethical issue arises for sex therapists in terms of goal setting when there are a variety of ways to conceptualize the problem (Brown & Sollod, 1988). Sexual issues and relationship issues coincide, leaving the sex therapist with the task of determining whether improvement within the sexual relationship will lead to improvements within the dyadic relationship, or whether changes to the dyadic relationship will improve the sexual problem. Some couples will entertain the notion that improvements may need to be made within their relationship before moving ahead with sex therapy; others, despite the therapist's beliefs regarding the etiology of the problem, are clear that the problem is only sexual and want to proceed immediately with sex therapy treatment. In such cases, the sex therapist needs to balance how to represent the feasibility of the client's goals while still engendering hope and confidence in the therapeutic process (Brown & Sollod, 1988).

Secrets in Therapy

There can be times when ethical issues related to seeing a couple in sex therapy may emerge. This situation is especially prone to happen when one partner is seen individually or communicates something to the therapist outside the session. A secret may be created within this context. For example, in one case, a client who called for treatment admitted to the therapist that she noted the orgasm problems began as a result of a fight she and her partner had, but that her partner believed the problem to be related to the medication she was taking. In another case, a client admitted to carrying on an affair and therefore knew that the sexual problems he was having were specific to his partner rather than generalized. Each of these scenarios must be managed delicately by a therapist to avoid becoming triangulated within the client system.

Schneider and Levinson (2006) outline the ethical issues related to the treatment of sex addicts within therapy specifically related to the disclosure of secrets in treatment. Three considerations for therapists are (1) what happens if the secret is revealed, (2) what happens if the secret is not disclosed, and (3) the effect on the therapist and therapeutic process if the secret is not disclosed. Therapists must also make a decision as to whether to see each member of the couple separately, the couple together, or a combination of the two. Schneider and Levinson believe that the therapist needs to address secrets that are relevant to the couple's therapy.

Weeks, Odell, and Methven (2005) provided an extensive discussion of the rules of confidentiality in treatment. The rule they suggested is based on the idea that confidence will be maintained so long as it does interfere with the progress of treatment. In some cases, one partner may need therapy in individual sessions apart from the partner. This partner must take responsibility for explaining why he or she needs the individual sessions. If there is a secret preventing progress, the partner in the individual sessions is requested to reveal the secret to his or her partner. If this is not done, then the therapist may also unilaterally stop therapy by telling the couple that an individual issue is preventing progress but not reveal the content of the secret. At this point, the other partner knows there is a secret and will choose whether to pursue learning what it might be. The utilization of this strategy is vastly more complex than described here. Readers searching for more options in dealing with secrets such as incest, infidelity, and so on should carefully examine our chapter on confidentiality in the text mentioned earlier.

Scope of Practice

We hope that this book has put forth the principles of sex therapy in a clear manner, enabling therapists to implement the strategies easily. However, "sex therapist" is a specialized term that implies a specific set of training, supervision, and clinical experience. Before advertising oneself as a sex therapist, one must go through the requisite credentialing process. Part of this includes 90 hours of human sexuality education, 60 clock hours of sex therapy training, 10 hours of value training, and 250 clinical hours of clinical experience of cases with sexual concerns (see the AASECT Web site for more details). A therapist must be clear with clients that, although he or she practices the principles of sex therapy, he or she is not a certified sex therapist and should be prepared to provide appropriate referrals in the area.

Referrals and Consultations in Sex Therapy

The number of qualified or certified professionals in sex therapy is few. In cases where a clinician need to refer to a sex therapist, he or she can visit the AASSCT Web site and select "for the public" and "locate a professional." A clickable map will appear where one can select one's area. The American Board of Sexology also certifies sex therapists and maintains an online site to locate board-certified sex therapists.

Sex therapists are almost always in a position of having to deal with multiple factors in the etiology of a sexual problem. They cannot work in isolation, but need to think of treatment in interdisciplinary terms. This fact requires the sex therapist to have many other human resources with whom he or she can collaborate closely. Sex therapists should build relationships with the following professionals, at least:

- obstetricians, gynecologists, and urologists;
- primary care physicians, internal medicine specialists, and psychiatrists;
- pain management physicians;
- psychologists; and
- clergy.

The sex therapist will probably need to educate the professional about the nature of sex therapy and the fact that multiple etiologies may be involved and interact with each other. The sex therapist is at the hub of treatment, coordinating the goals and interventions of the other professionals. Unfortunately, some professionals do not understand the value of a collaborative relationship or may want to take control of treatment in spite of the fact that the problem is outside their scope of practice. Building a therapeutic team is an essential part of being effective as a sex therapist.

Managing Ethical Dilemmas

Managing ethical dilemmas in sex therapy can be an overwhelming experience for the therapist. Ravella (2007) believes that therapists should consult with colleagues when an ethical question or situation arises. There are several opportunities for the sex therapist to obtain consultation. The therapist can, for example, obtain supervision or consultation from another certified sex therapist in the local area. The American Association for Sexuality Educators, Counselors and Therapists (AASECT) provides a directory of certified sex therapists in each state on its Web site. In cases where a certified sex therapist cannot be found locally, the therapist might also seek consultation from an already established clinical supervisor. Such a supervisor, although not a specialist in sex therapy, can provide consultation related to the relational dynamics and interventions and shed light on potential etiology and other general psychotherapy techniques and approaches. Finally, the therapist can seek consultation from other therapists in the area working with the same issues, developing a supportive and collaborative network.

The preceding issues are ethical issues because the therapist, in an attempt to understand and implement each person's perspective in the client identification, has to be very careful to avoid coalitions (Brown & Sollod, 1988; Hill & Coll, 1992). Each partner may feel justified in blaming the other, but that ultimately will not work toward effective problem resolution.

Sex Therapy Surrogates

The term "surrogate" in sex therapy refers to an individual who will engage in physical relations, frequently intimate sexual behaviors, with a client.* Surrogates commonly focus on building skills with emotional and sexual intimacy and social skills, relaxation, and sexual touching. In most circumstances, they are professionals who are enlisted to help clients overcome sexual dysfunction. They are frequently individuals who have gone through significant training, are certified in their profession, and work closely with sex therapists, counselors, and other similar professionals in the best interest of the client. In fact, sexual surrogates have their own professional organization, the International Professional Surrogates Association, with its own code of ethics, which can be viewed online at http://members.aol.com/Ipsa1/ethics.html. Masters and Johnson introduced the use of sexual surrogates into practice and developed a program utilizing the surrogates, though the surrogates in Masters and Johnson's program were always women used for men experiencing sexual issues (Bancroft, 1981; Brown & Sollod, 1988; Redlich, 1980). Other therapists have used both men and women as surrogates (Bancroft, 1981).

Ravella (2007) discusses the controversy around the implementation of surrogates in sex therapy. First, she advises therapists to be aware of and adhere to the laws governing the use of sex surrogates in their practice (Brown & Sollod, 1988). Another issue that needs consideration is the impact of involving a third party in the couple's sex therapy treatment. As many authors have pointed out (see, for example, Weeks & Gambescia, 2002), sex therapy can include aspects of couples counseling such as improving communication, addressing blocks to intimacy, and other issues related to relationship satisfaction. In this context, it may be difficult for the therapist, surrogate, and couple to untangle the relational/dyadic issues from the explicit sexual education and guidance issues for

---

* Sexual surrogates differ from facilitated sex in that facilitated sex refers to the assistance required by a disabled individual to assist with the preparation to participate in sexual activity, including positioning, removal of attire, etc. Unlike sexual surrogacy, the sexual facilitator does not participate in sexual activity.

which the surrogate has been hired to work. The use of surrogates may be seen as creating a breach in confidentiality (Redlich, 1980), particularly in relation to the other aspects of the couple's case (i.e., communication issues, etc.). What happens, for example, when a male client becomes attached to the surrogate and/or begins to share intimate details of his relationship with the surrogate? Redlich (1980) also suggests that another problem faced by the use of surrogates, despite training, may be that the client views the surrogate as a prostitute (Bancroft, 1981). In other cases, the surrogate may believe that he or she is in the same position as the therapist. As Brown and Sollod (1988) note:

> Perhaps in the future, the use of surrogates, as trained teachers of sexual skills, will be commonplace and acceptable. At the present time, however, due to legal and ethical considerations as well as practical problems, the use of surrogates cannot be recommended. (pp. 399–400)

Organizations and Guidelines for Ethical Issues in Sex Therapy

In discussing ethics in sex therapy, Ravella (2007) emphasizes the need for the therapist to understand the profession's code of ethics. The therapist has a responsibility to be familiar with the ethical codes that include the scope of practice and professional organizations to which he or she belongs. AASECT publishes its own code of ethics for the practice of sex therapy and sex education. The ethical code has been reprinted within VandeCreek, Peterson, and Bley's (2007) text, *Innovations in Clinical Practice: Focus on Sexual Health: Innovations in Clinical Practice,* as well as on the AASECT Web site at http://www.aasect.org/codeofethics.asp. This code establishes guidelines for the code of conduct in the areas of competence and integrity, ethical and moral standards, protection of the consumer, welfare of students and trainees, and welfare of research participants.

Because sex therapy also involves couples therapy, the therapist should be a member of the American Association of Marriage and Family Therapists (AAMFT) and should definitely be familiar with its code of ethics. This code can be found online at http://www.aamft.org/resources/LRMPlan/Ethics/ethicscode2001.asp. Ravella (2007) advises that, if a therapist is a member of more than one professional organization, he or she should follow the code of the organization that is more restrictive so as to err on the side of caution. Similarly, the Society for the Scientific Study of Sexuality (2007) has published an ethics statement that advises all members to follow the ethics guidelines of their disciplines.

Monitoring Biases in Treatment
Gender

A number of therapist variables operate in all types of therapy, including sex therapy. Gender biases "refer to biases associated with complex characteristics in biological, cultural, social, and political categories" (Guanipa & Woolley, 2000, p. 183). This is an unconscious factor in how therapists see and make interpretations about the world (Fisher, 1989). In other words, the therapist can be impacted by many social background characteristics, some of which he or she might be aware and others that he or she may not be aware of. The selection of therapeutic goals and therapist behavior may be influenced by therapist values (Brown & Sollod, 1988). "Even the diagnosis of sexual dysfunction, which appears at first to be objective and factual, is based in part on a complex chain of values and beliefs" (Brown & Sollod, 1988, p. 389). For example, orgasm in men was regarded more highly than women having orgasms; same-sex oriented individuals were viewed as pathological. As research and times have changed, the values of therapists around these issues (and hence the identification of problems and development of treatment strategies) have also shifted.

According to Wakefield (1987), sex bias occurs when "overpathologizing results from a sex-linked inequity in the way that a diagnostic criterion is formulated" (p. 465). Therapists who have different standards of pathology for men and women are essentially creating sex bias. Rieker and Carmen (1983) suggested that there is a double standard in mental health based on the sex role differences ascribed to sex role stereotyping and how one is adjusted to one's environment. Broverman, Vogel, Broverman, Clarkson, and Rosenkrantz (1972) found that the stereotype of a healthy woman, according to mental health practitioners, was different from the stereotype of a healthy man or a healthy adult. Healthy women were considered more submissive, less adventurous, more suggestive, less competitive, less logical, and less objective.

The implications of the Broverman et al. (1972) study might be that men and women get different treatment because there is a different view of what an appropriate outcome or healthy behavior would look like for both men and women. Sex therapists may find women who are aggressive about the initiation of sex as more pathological than women who are more submissive. Reiker and Carmen (1983) supported this finding when they stated that "anger in women is often labeled as pathological rather than understood as a consequence of a devalued position" (p. 29). A sex therapist might use different words for men and women to describe the same behavior. Sherman (1980, 1982) found that therapists' sex role values are operating during therapy: Therapists rated those individuals who are sex role discrepant as more maladjusted. However, Zygmond and Denton (1988) mailed questionnaires to members of the American Association for Marriage and Family Therapy and found that gender itself did not have a significant impact on the way clinicians chose to treat their clients. The reason their research differs from that of others is unclear.

Gender biases also have implications for problems that are not just major sexual dysfunctions. Hecker, Trepper, Wetchler, and Fontaine (1995) found that if a therapist believes that men tend to engage in infidelity more often than women and is seeing a couple in which a woman has engaged in infidelity, the therapist might view the women as more pathological because her behavior does not fit the norm. Hertlein (2004) investigated therapists' biases in the treatment of Internet infidelity cases. Although most therapists overtly reported that their treatment would not differ depending on the gender of the identified client, the data as a whole indicated the opposite.

Handy, Valentich, Cammaert, and Gripton (1985) highlight three main issues with regard to gender roles and implication for sex therapy. First, they report that there is the potential for sex therapists to be unaware that they are reinforcing gender roles. For example, a sex therapist may place a greater value on the man achieving orgasm in the relationship than the woman, stemming from the belief that this is more important to men. In the preceding example, the first interventions might be designed to manage the man's issue within treatment and give less priority to the woman's problems and goals. Finally, the sex therapist may miss critical issues in couples whose presentation is more androgynous than ingrained in sex role stereotypes. Handy et al. (1985) advise that sex therapists should conduct balanced assessments that give equal air time to the interests of both parties.

In other cases, the gender role reinforcement experienced by the couple in treatment is a reflection of the therapist's gender. Several studies have shown therapists treat sexual problems differently depending on the therapist's gender (i.e., Liss-Levinson, 1979; Schover, 1981; Schwartz & Strom, 1978). Schover (1981) examined therapists' responses to sexual material introduced by clients. Therapists were given case descriptions, photos, and audiotape of a client discussing a vague sexual symptom. Female therapists appeared to be more comfortable with sexual material than male therapists were; male therapists over- or underemphasized the sexual content.

Religion

Religious values of both the client and therapist can also affect the conceptualization of a sex therapy case (Brown & Sollod, 1988; Hertlein, 2004). Therapists who indicated that they were highly religious rated clients in vignettes regarding sexual behavior as more pathological than therapists who indicated lower levels of religiosity (Hecker et al., 1995). Therapists also viewed single persons engaging in intercourse with multiple partners as more pathological than those engaging in sex with the same frequency who were married. Hertlein (2004) found that more religious therapists were more likely to view clients in Internet infidelity scenarios as sex addicted, viewed the problem the couple was facing as more severe than therapists with lower levels of religiosity did, and found the presenting problems to be more damaging to the relationship. This impacted treatment because more religious therapists were more likely to suggest treatment focus on first-order change strategies and focus treatment on the individual rather than the couple.

Finally, Nijs (2006) discusses the difficulty sex therapists have in being objective within their work: "[T]he sex counselor or therapist cannot withdraw into a purely objective position. The sex counselor always remains involved as a person" (p. 124). Inherent in the role of a sex therapist is the constant involvement in the sexual problems of couples and individuals, and Nijs suggests that this can create difficulty in managing therapeutic burnout, stating that "Sex counselors and therapists can only care for patients or couples, if they care for themselves and each other" (p. 125). Strategies to combat this include having the couple highlight the positive experiences in a couple's life or history together as part of the therapeutic work (Nijs, 2006).

9

Formalized Assessments and Inventories in Sex Therapy

We are recorders and reporters of the facts—not judges of the behavior we describe.

Alfred Kinsey

Introduction

Assessment in sex therapy is a critical part of the therapeutic process. Information gathered in an assessment frequently results in how one conducts the treatment process, including guiding decisions in who participates in treatment, the structure of the sessions, and the interventions planned. Assessment in sex therapy can be formalized via the use of specific measures or instruments or be more informal, via the taking of a psychosocial history or examining behavior. This chapter provides an overview of a variety of assessments, both physiological and psychological. It presents reliability and validity information about current scales as well as a discussion of the relative strengths and weaknesses of the scales covered.

Behavioral Assessment

In addition to the information gained during a clinical interview, the therapist might also want to use some behavioral measures. These differ from the psychological measures in that the therapist relies on his or her observations of the client. In order to conduct a behavioral assessment, one needs to identify specific behaviors of interest and evaluate what dynamics or factors are maintaining those behaviors (Gudjonsson, 1986).

For example, the therapist can glean information regarding the couple's commitment, intimacy level, and passion toward one another from observations of how the couple interacts together in the session. The therapist can determine the necessity of a behavioral assessment based on the presenting problem, the severity of the problem, the couple's dynamics, and the goals of such an assessment.

Physiological Measures

There are a variety of physiological measures used by sexuality researchers and clinicians. For example, to monitor erectile dysfunction, penile circumference can be measured by the use of penile plethysmography (Simon & Schouten, 1991), of which there are two types: the volumetric air chamber, which measures changes through an assessment of the displacement of air around the penis, and the circumferential transducer, which measures changes in the circumference of the penis through a strain gauge placed around the shaft of the penis. Primarily, sexuality researchers have employed the use of the circumferential transducer. Although the physiological measures are intended to infer one's subjective state, more recent research has indicated that this is not always the case. For example, Delizonna, Wincze, Litz, Brown, and Barlow (2001) examined the physiological and subjective arousal indicators of 28 men without sexual dysfunction under two arousal conditions. They found that although there was evidence of penile tumescence, this was not necessarily accompanied by a subjective state of arousal. For further discussion of the nocturnal penile tumescence method, see Schiavi (1992).

In women, the complementary physiological measure is the vaginal photoplethysmography, which measures the amount of vasocongestion in the vaginal wall via the insertion of a "tampon" with a light source and a photocell. The amount of light that is produced is converted into electrical impulses and interpreted as an estimate of blood flow. Other researchers (i.e., Rogers, Van de Castle, Evans, & Critelli, 1985) have utilized an assessment of vaginal pulse amplitudes (measuring genital vasodilation) using the same device.

Another way that researchers have measured arousal physiologically is through assessing study participant reaction time (Letourneau, 2002; Williams, 2003). For example, Koukounas and McCabe (2001) assessed the interaction of sexual and emotional variables that influenced response to erotic material. They measured the reaction time it took participants to activate a switch after hearing a tone, as well as monitoring eye-blinking behavior as recorded by EMG activity. In other cases, skin conductance has also been used (Quinsey, Steinman, Bergersen, & Holmes, 1975) to measure arousal to sexual stimuli.

Psychological Measures

Researchers make wide use of standardized assessment instruments in the screening of sexual dysfunctions for clinical trials and in measuring treatment outcome during the medical and psychological treatment of sexual dysfunctions. These instruments generate scores for respondents' perceptions of sexual activities responses during the desire, arousal, and orgasm phases of the sexual response cycle, as well as respondents' satisfaction with, or pain during, these phases (Derogatis, 2008). Unfortunately, because these types of instruments are frequently designed for research, many do not have a strong application in clinical practice. Further, until insurance and HMOs reimburse for sexual dysfunctions, it is unlikely that sex therapists will be required to perform standardized assessments of their clients.

That said, there may be times when a formalized assessment is warranted in clinical practice. Ideally, standardized instruments will allow therapists to identify and diagnosis quickly, easily, and accurately, utilizing more or less agreed upon measures of sexual functioning. This section begins by addressing issues in the administration of standardized instruments in the private sex therapy practice. This section provides only a brief overview of a variety of assessments that address both individual and couple sexual dysfunction, reviewing some sources for instruments and providing a clinically useful chart listing the application (gender or issue), domains assessed, number of items and method of scoring, and psychometric properties for a variety of instruments.

Pion and Wagner (1971) report that the use of a questionnaire "is not to usurp the importance of data collection by the interview technique but rather to enhance this objective" (p. 3). The therapist should convey to the client that there is no "right" or "wrong" answer and encourage honesty in his or her responses.

Burg and Sprenkle (1996) advise that sexuality measures should assess from many perspectives (client, therapist, partner); however, self-report questionnaires are the most frequently used. Clinicians can frequently find complete inventories in journal articles or in books of collections of formalized assessments. Bancroft (1990) reports that some advantages of questionnaires include the potential for anonymity, standardization, and time saved compared to other assessment techniques.

Wincze and Carey (2001) outline strategies for clinicians to evaluate questionnaires. First, it is important to examine the psychometric properties of a questionnaire. Questionnaires that are used should have some evidence of adequate reliability and validity. Second, clinically relevant questionnaires should be selected. For example, some questionnaires are devoted to assessing many dimensions of sexuality, but other instruments only measure a few dimensions of sexual behavior. The key is for the therapist to have a clear understanding of his or her needs as well as the purpose of the inventory. Another consideration is the practicality of an inventory. In some cases, the reading level of the scale surpasses that of the client (Wincze & Carey, 2001). Two final considerations include comparability (i.e., how clients' scores compare to scores of others who took the test) and cost.

Conte (1983) divides the assessments into two classes: Guttman-type scales and scales looking at a wider range of behavior. Guttman-type scales, as defined by Conte, are those that are described as "cumulative and unidimensional" (p. 557). Typically, these scales are short in length (10–20 items). The second class of assessments is multidimensional, typically composed of more items, and measures a wider scope of behavior. Conte summarizes that unidimensional scales are useful for assessing behavior throughout the course of treatment, but he admits that such scales may have a higher degree of utility in research than clinical settings. Multidimensional scales are typically more comprehensive and might have greater utility in clinical settings in terms of treatment planning and outcome.

- unidimensional scales
  - Podell and Perkins (1957)
  - Brady and Levitt (1965)
  - Bentler (1968a, 1968b)
  - Zuckerman (1973)
  - Zuckerman, Tushup, and Finner (1976)
- multidimensional scales
  - Thorne (1966a, 1966b)
  - Marks and Sartorius (1967)
  - LoPiccolo and Steger (1974)
  - Harbison, Graham, Quinn, McAllister, and Woodward (1974)
  - Hoon et al. (1976)
  - Paitich, Langevin, Freeman, Mann, and Handy (1977)
  - Derogatis (1975)

Conte (1983) also provides two tables summarizing such scales. There has not been further classification in the literature of these scales in spite of the fact that his article was published over two decades ago.

Collections of Assessments

There are several ways to find psychological measures related to sexuality: in individual journal articles, in collections of sexual or dyadic assessments, or in works that focus on the treatment of a particular sexual dysfunction. For example, Schiavi, Derigotas, Kuriansky, O'Connor, and Sharpe (1979) summarized the assessment tools, lists, and descriptions of a variety of sexual assessment instruments. Although this article is nearly 30 years old, it provides detailed information about many of the tests and assessments that are still in use today, including information on obtaining the scale, method of administration, and reliability and validity information. Further, Talmadge and Talmadge (1990) also provide a review of assessments in sexuality geared toward clinical practice. They reviewed 14 different scales, including the Sexual Interaction Inventory, the Derigotas Sexual Functioning inventory, the Sexual Functioning Questionnaire for Heterosexuals, Sexual Orientation Method and Anxiety, and the Guttman Scale of Sexual Experience.

Another comprehensive review of the measures assessing one's quality of sex life is from Arrington, Cofrancesco, and Wu (2004). The authors found over 160 sexuality assessments that assessed quality of sexual life. They further divided the articles into three groups: articles with no reliability/validity listed, those that had reliability listed, but whose reliability was inadequate (below .70), and those with adequate reliability and validity. Further, the articles are divided into whether the inventory is a unidimensional measure (i.e., whether the scale was only intended to measure sexual quality of life) or whether the inventory is multidimensional, where only one subscale intends to measure sexual quality of life. The findings indicate that there were 62 instruments that represented six areas in sexual functioning: attitude, arousal, interest, desire, satisfaction, and relationship qualities. Yet, after sifting through the analysis, the authors found that only 9 of the 60+ measures displayed adequate validity and reliability.

Many sexual assessments are described in the most recent edition of the *Handbook of Sexuality-Related Measures* (Davis, Yarber, Bauserman, Schreer, & Davis, 1998). The text, which is approximately 600 pages, describes over 200 measures, which cover a variety of areas in sexual functioning, including measures to assess attitudes and beliefs about sexually charged topics, the presence of sexual dysfunctions, gender identity, masturbation, orgasm, etc. Meana, Binik, and Thaler (2006), however, state: "The comprehensiveness of this reference text is deceiving, however, as it creates the impression that the field of human sexuality is rich in assessment tools. In terms of sexual function and its clinical assessment, quite the opposite is true."

Indeed, our investigation revealed that the body of literature contains many assessment instruments that do not give adequate reliability and validity estimates. Those interested in reading descriptions on the wide body of instruments available are referred to the *Handbook of Sexuality-Related Measures,* Meana and colleagues' chapter in *A Guide to Assessments That Work* (2006), Schiavi, Derigotas, Kuriansky, O'Connor, and Sharpe's (1979) article, and Talmadge and Talmadge's (1990) article.

Meana et al. (2006) have written extremely useful critiques and reviews of assessment instruments. They discuss various methods to measure subjective and physiological sexual phenomena related to global sexual function. They describe each of the sexual dysfunctions in the *DSM-IV-TR* and review global sexual function measures that are appropriate to diagnosis, case conceptualization and treatment planning, and treatment monitoring and outcome. Their review focuses on scales that have adequate psychometric properties. The authors critique and evaluate the scales' norms, various types of reliability and validity, internal consistency, and an evaluation of clinical utility. The scales they investigated were divided into different groupings, such as inventories for couples, inventories for men, inventories for women, global inventories, and dysfunction-specific inventories.

The Derogatis Interview for Sexual Functioning (DISF; Derogatis, 1997, 1998) and the Golombok–Rust Inventory of Sexual Satisfaction (GRISS; Rust & Golombok, 1985, 1986, 1998) are scales that assess global functioning and are appropriate for either men or women. Of these two scales, neither was highly recommended by the authors, but the GRISS received higher ratings in several areas. The inventories reviewed for use for men were Brief Sexual Function Inventory—Male (BSFI-M; O'Leary et al., 1995), the International Index of Erectile Function (IIEF; Rosen et al., 1997), and the Male Sexual Health Questionnaire (MSHQ; Rosen, Lobo, Block, Yang, & Zipfel, 2004). Of these three, the IIEF was highly recommended by the authors.

The scales reviewed for use with women are the Brief Sexual Function Inventory for Women (BISF-W; Rosen, Taylor, & Leiblum, 1998; Taylor, Rosen, & Leiblum, 1994), Female Sexual Function Index (FSFI; Rosen et al., 2000), McCoy Female Sexuality Questionnaire (MFSQ; McCoy & Matyas, 1998), Sexual Function Questionnaire (SFQ; Quirk, Haughie, & Symonds, 2005; Quirk, Heiman, & Rosen, 2002), and the Structured Diagnostic Method (SDM; Utian et al., 2005). Of these, the scales most highly recommended by the authors were the FSFI, SFQ, and the MSFQ. Of the two dysfunction-specific scales (the Sexual Aversion Scale [SAS] and the IIEF), the IIEF was highly recommended by the authors, seemingly because of its norms' validity and generalizability.

Assessments in clinical practice and research have different aims. The clinician needs an inexpensive, nonthreatening, focused, and somewhat reliable method of beginning to understand a sexual problem. The clinician would continue assessment through a clinical interview and continue to collect assessment data as therapy unfolds. Assessment is a place for the clinician to begin, rather than serving as an end-point in a research study. As Meana et al. (2006) state: "The comprehensiveness … is deceiving, however, as it creates the impression that the field of human sexuality is rich in assessment tools. In terms of sexual function and its clinical assessment, quite the opposite is true."

10

Handouts, Exercises, and Worksheets

Introduction

The purpose of this chapter is to give the reader some of the basic tools, skills, and resources to be successful in sex therapy. We will be covering the topics of handouts, sensate-focus exercises, genograms, and homework. Our intent is to give readers the practical information they need to implement the treatment strategies described earlier in this volume. We would like to remind the reader once again that all sensate focus and homework exercises are to be performed with the attitude of learning to give and receive pleasure and should be balanced so that each partner receives something he or she wants. The early literature and much of the recent literature fail to recognize the systemic nature of these exercises. The systemic nature of sex therapy is emphasized throughout this volume and in all our earlier work referenced here.

Handouts

The recent publication, *Innovations in Clinical Practice: Focus on Sexual Health* (Vandecreek, Peterson, & Bley, 2007), provides several handouts for use in sex therapy for both the therapist and the client. Therapist handouts are generally designed to provide the therapist assistance in treatment planning; client handouts are designed to help clients examine attitudes and beliefs, become better educated on a topic, or practice different skills. For the therapist, an example would be Peterson's (2007) handout representing a sexual identity cube. It is based on the work of Kinsey, Bem, and Money. It depicts a $3 \times 3 \times 3$ cube with three planes:

one plane describing a client's sexual orientation (heterosexual, bisexual, or homosexual), another describing gender (male, transgender, female), and one plane identifying the client's sex role (masculine, androgynous, feminine). This tool helps the therapist better identify clients' perceptions of their sexuality.

In terms of handouts for the clients, an example would be Bley's (2007a, 2007b) handouts that guide sensate-focus activities and pelvic floor exercises. These handouts describe, in brief and concise terms, how to implement the exercises. The sensate focus handout guides the couple through three stages of activities: nongenital pleasuring, nongenital and genital pleasuring, and intercourse pleasuring. Also included in the handout are the "go slow" messages that should be provided during the implementation of sensate-focus activities.

Exercises

Sensate-Focus Activities

One of the most common exercises in sex therapy is the use of what has been termed the sensate focus or pleasuring exercises. Sensate focus refers to a set of nondemanding, pleasuring exercises beginning with nonthreatening, nongenital experiences. As the exercises progress, sensate-focus exercises ultimately allow the couple to participate in sexually pleasuring activities paired with relaxation. This exercise is the practical application of systematic desensitization techniques in order to reduce the anxiety related to sexual interactions. Masters and Johnson delineated five levels of sensate focus (Charlton & Brigel, 1997): (1) nondemand touching and caressing without the breasts, (2) caressing including breasts but excluding genitals, (3) caressing including genitals, (4) penis in the vagina, and (5) intercourse excluding orgasm.

De Villers and Turgeon (2005) also provide specific guidelines for the implementation of sensate-focus activities into sex therapy. First, they advise that therapists may notice an increase in anxiety initially when implementing sensate-focus activities rather than a decrease in anxiety. Proper implementation will decrease anxiety over exercises. Timing and the actual directives given by the therapist are also important considerations. As with any activity or intervention, application similar to a "cookbook" approach not tailored to the client may not be as effective as interventions tailored to the client.

Some clients may move more quickly through the sensate-focus activities than others. In cases where the etiology of a sexual dysfunction can be attributed to multiple factors (i.e., physiology, individual psychology factors, couple/dyadic factors, family-of-origin factors, and/or sociocultural factors), the ability to complete the activities may take a longer amount of time than in cases where the etiology is rather straightforward. This fact is an important consideration because, by the time the couple gets to treatment, they have probably experienced many failed sexual encounters and will be very sensitive to doing any exercise likely to produce another failure. For this reason, sex therapists are encouraged to provide "go slow" messages to couples. This might include a "ban" on intercourse or other sexual activities within the course of treatment (Gambescia & Weeks, 2007), particularly for those couples experiencing orgasmic or desire disorders (Borrelli-Kerner & Bernell, 1997; Charlton & Brigel, 1997).

De Villers and Turgeon (2005) summarize caressing exercises for couples that can be incorporated into sex therapy and sensate focus activities. This includes instructions on how to perform appropriate hand caressing, foot caressing, and face caressing. They suggest that it is only after the caressing becomes comfortable and enjoyable to the couple that they should proceed with other sensate-focus techniques. The couple can then embark on caressing exercises that create anticipation and desire, which include undressing and slow, gentle hand placements.

According to Hertlein, Weeks, and Gambescia (2008), "Sensate focus homework increases the sense of cohesion, love, caring, commitment, cooperation, and intimacy between partners." Hertlein et al. describe the multiple functions of sensate focus and how to implement the exercises properly. It is the most highly articulated system of sensate focus in the literature. Whereas most approaches to sensate focus break it into two major exercises, Hertlein et al. also discuss the slow incremental development of exercises in collaboration with the clients in order to avoid the resistance that is often met in follow through. As a result, the process they describe could involve a few exercises or as many as needed in order to meet the goals that have been established.

Homework

One of the hallmark aspects of sex therapy is that of using homework to effect change. Homework can be helpful in sex therapy because learning can occur best by practice. Obviously, sexual activities are best completed by couples privately (Charlton & Brigel 1997; Gambescia & Weeks, 2007). Charlton and Brigel (1997) suggest that homework assignments in sex therapy should have components that attend to the emotions and to behaviors. Gambescia and Weeks (2007) believe that the therapist should play a "directive role in session and beyond the therapy hour through the judicious use of assignments to be performed at home" (p. 354). As a way to facilitate homework assignments, Gambescia and Weeks advise that the therapist work with couples to address their concerns related to homework completion. In many cases, these concerns relate to fear of failure and uncertainty about what to expect during the homework. The therapist should talk with the couple about their reactions to completing homework and may find it valuable to label homework as "tasks" or "exercises."

Like any other assignment in treatment, couples are more likely to comply if they feel that they have a vested interest in the process. The couple needs to understand the reason for the homework and can link the completion of the assignment to reaching their treatment goals. Each homework assignment is tailored to each couple. The creation of the exercises is always done collaboratively, with close attention given to clients' readiness to do the exercise and their ability to carry out the exercise. The exercise is always intended to produce success, not failure. The goal of the homework is to help the couple slowly reach their goal by keeping anxiety low and success high, and explaining each link in the chain as a step toward their goal. In a recent chapter, Gambescia and Weeks (2007) outlined some common homework assignments for specific sexual problems. See their work for a complete discussion of the various techniques and implementation of the assignments.

Panchana and Sofronoff (2005) suggested that although tailoring homework assignments to couples in sex therapy is important, there are also common structural elements that have been identified by many authors. For example, Weeks and Gambescia (2002) suggested that homework compliance is increased when the therapist and couple negotiate when the homework is to be scheduled, identify who will initiate the homework, and understand clearly what they are supposed to do within the homework. They considered some of the basic structural elements to be time, place, duration, and who is to do what.

Tompkins (2004) noted some common structural elements to successful homework. We have incorporated these into the guidelines that follow:

1. *Assign relevant, acceptable, and appropriate homework.* The homework should be viewed by the couple as relevant to meeting their goal. It should be a task that they deem as sexually acceptable. For example, the therapist would not prescribe an assignment that the couple had an aversion to doing. Both the therapist and the client should agree that the homework is appropriate to their meeting their goals. In addition, Gambescia and Weeks (2007) advise that the therapist work with couples to address their concerns related to homework completion. In many cases, these concerns relate to fear of failure and uncertainty about what to expect during the course of treatment. The therapist should talk with the couple about their reactions to completing homework and may find it valuable to label homework as "tasks" or "exercises." The therapist should discuss the emotional reaction to the homework after giving it rather than after the couple may have failed to do it. The couple's initial emotional reaction to a homework assignment is a good indication of their readiness for or their resistance to doing it.

   We have provided a complete list of books, videos, Web sites, and reputable adult stores in Chapter 11. Whenever a couple is told to read a particular book, watch a video, etc., the therapist should use the same procedure described earlier that involves asking them how they feel about each activity. A classic example is when the therapist suggests buying a vibrator when treating inorgasmia. This suggestion can stir powerful feelings on both sides and may need to be processed thoroughly and slowly.

2. *Make sure the homework is appropriate to the couple's age, ability, and lifestyle.* The homework should match the clients' physical abilities and be considerate of their resources, including free time, schedules, and finances. Typically, the couple is asked to do the homework assignment three times during any given week. The couple must be ready (state of willingness) to begin the homework and have the time available to devote to its completion. Suggesting that an economically strapped couple go on a second honeymoon for a week or buy an expensive vibrator merely sets them up for failure The therapist should always ensure that the couple is capable of doing the homework, paying attention to any physical limitations based on health problems, age, and ability to get the required resources.

3. *Assign simple, clear homework with specific instructions.* It may be helpful for the therapist to develop assignments with the clients and to take a collaborative attitude in designing the homework. The couple can be given the parameters of the exercise and asked to think about how and when they would like to do it. This gives them a sense of ownership in their therapy.

4. *Start small and build on successes.* The therapist should begin with simple homework exercises and work toward more difficult, complex, or challenging ones as defined by the couple. As we stated earlier, the purpose of the homework is to build one successful experience at a time. For a more detailed discussion of success in sex therapy treatment, see Trepper, Treyger, Yalowitz, and Ford (2008).

5. *Make assignments single focused and specific.* The therapist should make sure the assignment is specific and directs either behavioral or attitudinal changes and not allow ambiguity or veiled references to muddy the focus of the assignment. The language used in making the assignment should be direct, clear, concise, behavioral, and understandable to the couple. The couple needs to focus on only one step at a time. For example, the therapist might start with a behavioral exercise of monitoring what happens to obtain a behavioral baseline. The next step might be to engage in some touching behavior in the living room and the next to touching each other fully clothed in bed. This sequence of exercises helps the couple reconnect physically through specific steps.

6. *Ensure understanding.* The therapist should ask the couple to write down the homework or repeat it back to make sure they both agree to do it and understand the purpose of the exercise before they leave the session. For high-conflict couples or those who may have motivation not to complete the homework, a homework contract should be created. The terms of the contract should be reviewed with each partner and each should sign it. The therapist makes three copies, giving one to each partner and placing the third in their chart. We believe this task is appropriate but do not agree that creating a contract is likely to make the assignment happen. Our view is to deal with the relational issues first as well as discuss their readiness and emotions about doing the homework.

7. *Obtain an investment.* Clients should be asked how they feel about the assignment, what problems they might have in doing it, and, in some cases, how they might sabotage the exercise. It might help to phrase the assignment as a "win–win" situation. The therapist should ask each partner what he or she thinks the exercise will offer him or her individually and as part of a couple. For example, the exercise might be designed so that each partner is to do something different. For one partner, the goal may be therapeutic, while for the other it is simply pleasurable. The therapist needs to make sure that each partner feels that his or her role in the homework is important, enjoyable, and worthwhile.

8. *Build in contingency plans and offer flexibility.* Part of ensuring buy-in is to give the couple options in completing the assignment. Planning for unforeseen circumstances lets the couple know that the therapist understands and appreciates the complexity of their lives. More importantly,

it emphasizes the process in which they become more sexual with each other over the outcome of a "completed assignment."

9. *Offer support.* The couple should be told to call the therapist midweek if they have questions or are confused about the assignment as they undertake it. Most couples will not need this step, but if they do, it can almost always be handled quickly. They also feel that the therapist cares about their treatment more if he or she makes this offer.

The discussion or processing of an assignment can be just as valuable as the assignment itself. Therefore, some key issues need to be considered when addressing homework. One issue is to follow up regularly. Therapists should always follow up on the exercise at the beginning of the next session. The more consistently therapists review homework, the more seriously the clients will take, and undertake, it. In reviewing homework, the therapist needs to keep in mind the "three As":

Ask for details. The therapist should get a specific description of what happened each time from each partner. They should be forewarned that the therapist will be asking them about all their homework and to keep mental or written records. Some sex therapists encourage their clients to get a calendar with big space for writing or a dated journal where they record their efforts. This information will enable the therapist to gauge their progress and design the next exercise.

Address efforts. Some couples may have difficulty with even the most basic exercise. The therapist should be sure to stay positive and validate whatever efforts they made in completing the homework. He or she can find and share with them any changes observed in their attitudes or behaviors, giving consistent praise and encouragement. If it appears that one partner has had more success in homework completion than the other has, the therapist should be sure to stay balanced by focusing on the teamwork nature of the exercises and paying attention to the process by which they undertook the homework as well as the outcome.

Anticipate incompletion. If the couple fails to do the exercise, then the therapist should process the reasons why and either proceed with the same exercise or work through their resistance. Some of the resistance might be related to their fears (for a detailed discussion, see Chapter 6). In some couples, relational issues such as couple conflict will prevent them from being successful in completing the homework. These must be worked on first. Other clients may have anticipated that any attempt to connect physically would result in anger, disappointment, a sense of failure, or any other negative feelings associated with sexual interaction in the past and thus avoided the attempt. If that is the case, then the therapist should work through the fears as he or she encourages their efforts to try the homework again.

In conclusion, all the material in this chapter adds to the therapist's repertoire of tools and skills. The skillful use of these tools is much easier to read about than to master. The best way to master this material is under the supervision of an experienced and credentialed sex therapist. The techniques and skills needed to do sex therapy appear deceptively simple. We have the misfortune of having treating many couples who have had a failed experience with an inexperienced, unsupervised, and noncredentialed sex therapist. The most important tools any therapist can have are good academic training, workshops, lectures at sex therapy conferences, and, most of all, excellent supervision.

11

Psychoeducational Resources in Sex Therapy

Bibliotherapy

The use of bibliotherapy has been well documented in sex therapy (see, for example, Weeks & Gambescia, 2002). Bibliotherapy involves the use of material to stimulate new thoughts or actions in our clients. It could involve reading books or Internet-based material, viewing tapes, or watching selected TV shows or any form of media that would be considered psychoeducational. Of course, the most common connotation of bibliotherapy is that of reading books, although other forms of educational media are rapidly growing. Bibliotherapy should have the effect of helping to dispel misinformation, providing accurate information, giving couples new perspectives (attitudes), supporting trying new behaviors, suggesting new ideas or things they had not thought about, giving them permission to try "forbidden" behaviors, and many more functions.

Couples in sex therapy often feel that they are the only ones with the type of problem they have. They feel alone and isolated, and they over-pathologize their situation. They also feel embarrassed, confused, hopeless, and ashamed that they must reveal such intimate details to a stranger. Bibliotherapy has the potential to open the communication around the couple's problem area. Reading about a particular topic can help to desensitize couples to discussion topics. For example, most couples do not want to discuss their sexual fantasies. After reading one or more books on sexual fantasies, couples are usually much more open to discussing this topic. The mere fact that someone is writing about their problem has the effect of helping to normalize their behavior. They no longer feel alone in having the problem and may gain some useful insight and information about the nature of their problem. This normalizing function will help the couple to see that many individuals go through similar issues and have dealt with these issues successfully.

Appendix A lists some bibliotherapeutic resources that can be helpful to the client in sex therapy. Although this list is far from exhaustive, we believe that these resources are a basic starting point for therapists looking to assign bibliotherapy to their clients. These books cut across a wide variety of presenting problems and issues specific to sex therapy.

Videos and Multimedia

Videos and multimedia can provide a great deal of psychoeducation for clients struggling with sexual issues. Most of the videos listed here give tips and suggestions to couples on how to enhance their love-making. Many of these videos can be ordered through a variety of Web sites. Table 11.1 provides a list of some of the better resources for couples in sex therapy. This list reflects a few of the more traditional video selections assigned by therapists.

Internet Resources

There are also several major Internet sites that refer the reader to further information on books, films, and so on. These sites are major national organizations, research institutes, or clearinghouses for information. For example, therapists can refer clients to the American Association of Sexuality Educators, Counselors, and Therapists (AASECT) Web site (located at http://www.aasect.org), which has a section of links and resources available to the public (located at http://www.aasect.org/assoclinks.asp). This Web site provides links to such resources, including (but not limited to):

- American Association for Marriage and Family Therapy
- Foundation for the Scientific Study of Sexuality
- GLBT World
- The Kinsey Institute
- National Council on Family Relations
- SexandRelationships.com
- Sinclair Intimacy Institute
- Society for Sex Therapy and Research
- Women's Sexual Health Foundation

TABLE 11.1 Sexual Enhancement Videos

Video title/series name	Publisher/ producer	Where to get it
Better Sex video series	Sinclair Institute	Advertised on the Better Sex Web site at http://www.bettersex.com/Adult-Sex-Education/movie-collections/sp-better-sex-video-series-6-volume-collection-2313.aspx
Sex Essentials series	Victory Multimedia	Advertised on the Sex Essentials Web site at http://www.seductivesexpositions.com/
Loving Sex series	Alexander Institute	Advertised on the Loving Sex Web site at http://www.lovingsex.com/loving_sex.php
Becoming Orgasmic DVD	Sinclair Institute	Advertised on the Sinclair Institute Web site at http://www.store.sinclairinstitute.com/IBS/SimpleCat/Product/asp/hierarchy/0100/product-id/36818365.html
Great Sex for a Lifetime	Sinclair Institute	Advertised on the Sinclair Institute Web site at http://www.store.sinclairinstitute.com/IBS/SimpleCat/Product/asp/hierarchy/0100/product-id/36818365.html
Guide to Great Sex for Couples Over 40	Sinclair Institute	Advertised on the Sinclair Institute Web site at http://www.store.sinclairinstitute.com/IBS/SimpleCat/Product/asp/hierarchy/0T/product-id/3664573.html
The Big O	Sinclair Institute	Advertised on the Sinclair Institute Web site at http://www.store.sinclairinstitute.com/IBS/SimpleCat/Product/asp/product-id/3664577.html
Female Masturbation series	Welcomed Concensus	Advertised on the Welcomed Concensus Web site at http://www.welcomed.com/videos/video_fm.html
Deliberate orgasm	Welcomed Concensus	Advertised on the Welcomed Concensus Web site at http://www.welcomed.com/videos/video_do.html
Loving With Passion	Body, Mind, & Intimacy	Advertised on the Body, Mind, & Intimacy online store at http://www.loveandintimacy.com/lovwitpas.html
Better Sex video series for black couples	Sinclair Institute	Advertised on the Better Sex Web site at http://www.bettersex.com/Adult-Sex-Education/movie-collections/sp-the-better-sexvideo-series-for-black-couples-vol-1-2-set-282.aspx
Complete Guide to Sexual Positions	Pacific Media	Advertised on the Amazon Web site at http://www.amazon.com/Complete-Guide-Sexual-Positions-Assorted/dp/B00014NFDY
101 Love Positions	Body, Mind, & Intimacy	Advertised on the Body, Mind, & Intimacy online store at http://www.loveandintimacy.com/101lovpos.html

There are also places where couples can be referred to books related to sexuality and sexual health. For example, the Web site for the group Sex Therapy in Philadelphia provides a list of books for clients on a range of topics located at http://www.sextherapyinphiladelphia.com/sexual_self_help_books.htm. The topics covered on this site include communication, divorce, infidelity, sexual addiction, sexual orientation and gender, masturbation, sexual toys, and others. In addition, the Institute for Sexual and Marital Therapy has a Web site (located at http://www.sexualtherapy.com/) that provides a book list under the link "Bookstore" on its Web page (direct link: http://www.sexualtherapy.com/tools.htm). These books are recommended by the Web site authors and include areas related to human sexuality, sexual dysfunction, relationship issues, and information specifically geared toward men and women. There are also sites whose purpose is devoted to sexual enrichment. For example, Robert Birch offers a site designed to enhance sexual pleasure of adults. Located at http://www.oral-caress.com/, this site includes adult erotica and information about sexual techniques and provides resources for clients.

Some clients lack the basic terminology or language of sexuality. They do not know the names of various parts of the sexual anatomy or the proper lay terms for various behaviors. This fact may result in embarrassment in discussing some topics because they only know slang. In some cases, clients will not bring up a topic of concern due to their inadequate terminology. These clients can be directed to sites that help them learn more about the language of sex, including:

- University of Hawaii AIDS Educational and Training Center: http://www.hawaii.edu/hivandaids/links_sexterms.htm
- Farlex Dictionary of Sexual Terms and Expressions: http://www.sex-lexis.com/
- MyPleasure.Com/Sexology's Sex Glossary: http://www.sexology.org/glossary/glossary2.htm
- The Sex Dictionary: http://www.thesexdictionary.com/

The Internet has become a major and readily available source of practically free information. The therapist might search the Web to find a factually based Web site that addresses the need for information and then direct the client to it. More technologically sophisticated clients can be directed to do their own search with the caution that the Web site is part of some major (professional) organization or a university-based Web site. These sites will usually be up to date and contain factual information. The therapist needs to follow up to find out which sites the clients visited and what they learned. Information taken from the site should be assessed for its accuracy or relevance for the couple. The Internet can also provide an overwhelming amount of sexually stimulating photographs and film clips for couples simply interested in something to arouse them. Couples who are interested in sadomasochism (S and M) or bondage and discipline (B and D) may find little in the local bookstore, but a search on Amazon.com or the Internet will offer up plenty of material.

In conclusion, psychoeducational material is an invaluable resource for couples. The therapist should be familiar with the basic information in this chapter by reading or skimming the books, watching tapes, and visiting a variety of Web sites. Attending the book store at an AASECT conference gives the therapist an opportunity to view much of this material as well as see many of the sexual enhancement products (lubricants, sex toys, etc.) that are mentioned in another chapter. We assume that the therapist has attended a sexual attitude readjustment (SAR) workshop at a national conference or one offered privately in order to become desensitized to the vast spectrum of sexual behavior, language, and images he or she will encounter in clients and in the media and with which he or she should be familiar.

Appendix A: Bibliotherapy Resources

Barbach, L., & Levine, L. (1980). *Shared intimacies.* New York: Anchor Books.

Barbach, L. G. (1976). *For yourself: The fulfillment of female sexuality.* Garden City, NY: Doubleday.

Barbach, L. G. (1983). *For each other: Sharing sexual intimacy.* New York: NAL.

Comfort, A. (1994). *The new joy of sex: A gourmet guide to lovemaking in the nineties.* Westminster, MD: Random House Inc.

Comfort, A., & Rubenstein, J. (1992). *The new joy of sex: A gourmet guide to lovemaking in the nineties.* New York: Pocket Books.

De Villers, L. (2002). *A fun, upbeat guide to sex-cessful relationships* (2nd ed.). Marina Del Ray, CA: Aphrodite Media.

Foley, S., Kope, S. A., & Sugrue, D. P. (2001). *Sex matters for women: A complete guide to taking care of your sexual self.* New York: Guilford Press.

Friday, N. (1973). *My secret garden: Women's sexual fantasies.* New York: Pocket Books.

Friday, N. (1975). *Forbidden flowers: More women's sexual fantasies.* New York: Pocket Books.

Heiman, J. R., & LoPiccolo, J. (1992). *Becoming orgasmic: A sexual and personal growth program for women.* New York: Simon & Schuster.

Katz, D., & Tabisel, R. L. (2002). *Private pain: It's about life, not just sex ... understanding vaginismus & dyspareunia.* Plainview, NY: Women's Therapy Center.

Ladas, A. K., Whipple, B., & Perry, J. D. (2005). *The G spot.* New York: Dell Publishing.

Metz, M. E., & McCarthy, B. W. (2004a). *Coping with erectile dysfunction: How to regain confidence and enjoy great sex.* Oakland, CA: New Harbringer Publications.

Metz, M. E., & McCarthy, B. W. (2004b). *Coping with premature ejaculation: How to overcome PE, please your partner and have great sex.* Oakland, CA: New Harbringer Publications.

Milsten, R., & Slowinski, J. (1999). *The sexual male: Problems and solutions.* New York: Norton.

Zilbergeld, B. (1992). The man behind the broken penis: Social and psychological determinants of erectile failure. In R. C. Rosen & S. R. Leiblum (Eds.), *Erectile disorders: Assessment and treatment* (pp. 27–51). New York: Guilford Press.

Zilbergeld, B. (1999). *The new male sexuality.* New York: Random House.

Zilbergeld, B., & Ullman, J. (1984). *Male sexuality: A guide to sexual fulfillment.* New York: Bantam Books.

References

Adams, S., Dubbert, P., Chupurdia, K., Adolph Jones, J., Lofland, K., & Leermakers, E. (1996). Assessment of sexual beliefs and information of aging couples with sexual dysfunction. *Archives of Sexual Behavior, 25*(3), 249–260.

APA (American Psychiatric Association). (2000). *Diagnostic and statistical manual of mental disorders: Text revision* (4th ed.). Washington, DC: Author.

Arrington, R., Confrancesco, J., & Wu, A. W. (2004). Questionnaires to measure sexual quality of life. *An International Journal of Quality of Life Aspects of Treatment, 13*(10), 1643–1658.

Bancroft, J. (1981). Ethical aspects of sexuality and sex therapy. In S. Bloch & P. Chodoff (Eds.), *Psychiatric ethics* (pp. 160–184). New York: Oxford University Press.

Bancroft, J. (1990). Sexual behavior. In D. F. Peck & C. M. Colin (Eds.), *Measuring human problems: A practical guide* (pp. 339–373). Oxford, England: John Wiley & Sons.

Bancroft, J., & Janssen, E. (2000). The dual control model of male sexual response: A theoretical approach to centrally mediated erectile dysfunction. *Neuroscience and Biobehavioral Reviews, 24*, 571-579.

Basson, R., Berman, J., & Burnett, A. (2001). Report of the International Consensus Development Conference on Female Sexual Dysfunction: Definitions and classifications. *Journal of Sex and Marital Therapy, 27*(2), 83–94.

Barbach, L. (2000). *For yourself: The fulfillment of female sexuality.* New York: New American Library.

Bentler, P. M. (1968a). Heterosexual behavior assessment: I males. *Behavior Research and Therapy, 6*(1), 21–25.

Bentler, P. M. (1968b). Heterosexual behavior assessment: II females. *Behavior Research and Therapy, 6*(1), 27–30.

Berman, E. (1999). Gender, sexuality, and romantic love genograms. In R. DeMaria, G. Weeks, & L. Hof (Eds.), *Focused genograms: Intergenerational assessment of individuals, couples, and families* (pp. 145–176). New York: Brunner/Mazel.

Berman, E., & Hof, L. (1987). The sexual genogram—Assessing family-of-origin factors in the treatment of sexual dysfunction. In G. Weeks & L. Hof (Eds.), *Integrating sex and marital therapy: A clinical guide* (pp. 37–56). New York: W. W. Norton.

Bettinger, M. (2001). *It's your hour: A guide to queer affirmative psychotherapy.* Los Angeles: Alyson.

Bettinger, M. (2004). A systems approach to sex therapy with gay male couples. In J. Bigner & J. Wetchler (Eds.), *Relationship therapy with same-sex couples* (pp. 65–74). New York: The Haworth Press, Inc.

Bigner, J., & Wetchler, J. (2004). *Relationship therapy with same-sex couples.* New York: Haworth Press.

Bley, J. W. (2007a). Kegel exercises (pelvic floor exercises). In L. VandeCreek, F. L. Peterson, & J. W. Bley (Eds.), *Innovations in clinical practice: Focus on sexual health* (pp. 321–322). Sarasota, FL: Professional Resource Press/Professional Resource Exchange.

Bley, J. W. (2007b). Sexual pleasuring (sensate focus exercises). In L. VandeCreek, F. L. Peterson, & J. W. Bley (Eds.), *Innovations in clinical practice: Focus on sexual health* (pp. 317–320). Sarasota, FL: Professional Resource Press/ Professional Resource Exchange.

Borrelli-Kerner, S., & Bernell, B. (1997). Couple therapy of sexual disorders. In R. S. Charlton (Ed.) *Treating sexual disorders,* (pp.165-199). San Francisco: Jossey-Bass.

Brady, J. P., & Levitt, E. E. (1965). Scalability of sexual experiences. *Psychological Record, 15*(2), 275–279.

Brock, G., Nehra, A., Lipshultz, L., Karlin, G., Gleave, M., Seger, M., & Padma-Nathan, H. (2003). Safety and efficacy of Vardenafil for the treatment of men with erectile dysfunction after radical retropubic prostatectomy. *Journal of Urology, 4,* 1278–1283.

Broverman, I., Vogel, S., Broverman, D., Clarkson, F., & Rosenkrantz, P. (1972). Sex-role stereotypes: A current appraisal. *Journal of Social Issues, 28,* 59–78.

Brown, R., & Sollod, R. (1988). Ethical and professional issues in sex therapy. In R. Brown & J. Field (Eds.), *Treatment of sexual problems in individual and couples therapy* (pp. 387–408). Costa Mesa, CA: PMA Publishing Corp.

Burg, J. E., & Sprenkle, D. H. (1996). Sex therapy. In F. P. Piercy, D. H. Sprenkle, & J. L. Wetchler (Eds.), *Family therapy sourcebook* (2nd ed., pp. 153–180). New York: Guilford Press.

CACREP (2001). 2001 Standards. Council for Accreditation of Counseling and Related Educational Programs. Retrieved March 17, 2006, from http://www.cacrep.org/2001Standards.html#3

Camacho, M. E., & Reyes-Ortiz, C. A. (2005). Sexual dysfunction in the elderly: Age or disease? *International Journal of Impotence Research, 17,* S52–S56.

Carson, C. (2002). Erectile dysfunction in the 21st century: Whom we can treat, whom we cannot treat and patient education. *International Journal of Impotence Research, 14*(supplement 1), s29–s34.

Case, E., & Robinson, N. (1990). Toward integration: The changing world of family therapy. *American Journal of Family Therapy, 18,* 153–160.

Catalan, J., & Meadows, J. (2000). Sexual dysfunction in gay and bisexual men with HIV infection: Evaluation, treatment and implications. *AIDS Care, 12*(3), 279–286.

Cawood, E., & Bancroft, J. (1996). Steroid hormones, the menopause, sexuality and well-being of women. *Psychological Medicine, 26,* 925–936.

Charlton, R. S., & Brigel, F.W. (1997). Treatment of arousal and orgasmic disorders. In R. S. Charlton (Ed.), *Treating sexual disorders* (pp. 237–280). San Francisco: Jossey-Bass.

COAMFTE (2002). Standards of accreditation, version 10.3. American Association for Marriage and Family Therapy. Retrieved February 16, 2006, from http://www.aamft.org/about/COAMFTE/standards_of_accreditation.asp

Compton, W. M., & Cottier, L. B. (2004). The diagnostic interview schedule (DIS). In M. J. Hilsenroth & D. L. Segal (Eds.), *Comprehensive handbook of psychological assessment, Vol 2: Personality assessment* (pp. 153–162). Hoboken, NJ: John Wiley & Sons Inc.

Conte, H. R. (1983). Development and use of self-report techniques for assessing sexual functioning: A review and critique. *Archives of Sexual Behavior, 12*(6), 555–576.

Crenshaw, T., & Goldberg, J. (1996). *Sexual pharmacology: drugs that affect sexual function.* New York: W. W. Norton.

Damon, W., & Rosser, B. R. S. (2005). Anodyspareunia in men who have sex with men: Prevalence, predictors, consequences and the development of *DSM* diagnostic criteria. *Journal of Sex and Marital Therapy, 31,* 129–141.

Davis, C. M., Yarber, W. L., Bauserman, R., Schreer, G., & Davis, S. L. (Eds.). (1998). *Handbook of sexuality-related measures.* Thousand Oaks, CA: Sage Publications.

Delizonna, L. L., Wincze, J. P., Litz, B. T., Brown, T. A., & Barlow, D. H. (2001). A comparison of subjective and physiological measures of mechanically produced and erotically produced erections (or, is an erection an erection?). *Journal of Sex and Marital Therapy, 27*(1), 21–31.

DeMaria, R., Weeks, G., & Hof, L. (1999). *Focused genograms: Intergenerational assessment of individuals, couples, and families.* New York: Brunner/Mazel.

Dennerstein, L. (1996). Well-being, symptoms and the menopausal transition. *Maturitas, 23,* 147–157.

Dennerstein, L., Dudley, C., Hopper, J., & Burger, H. (1997). Sexuality, hormones and the menopausal transition. *Maturitas, 26,* 83–93.

Derby, C., Araujo, A., Johannes, C., Feldman, H., & McKinlay, J. (2000). Measurement of erectile dysfunction in population-based studies: The use of a single question self-assessment in the Massachusetts Male Aging Study. *International Journal of Impotence Research, 12,* 197–204.

Derogatis, L. R. (1975). *Derogatis sexual functioning inventory.* Baltimore, MD: Clinical Psychometrics Research.

Derogatis, L. R. (1997). The Derogatis interview for sexual functioning (DISF/DISF-SR): An introductory report. *Journal of Sex & Marital Therapy, 23,* 291–304.

Derogatis, L. R. (1998). The Derogatis interview for sexual functioning. In C. M. Davis, W. L. Yarber, R. Bauserman, G. Schreer, & S. L. Davis (Eds.), *Handbook of sexuality-related measures* (pp. 268–269). Thousand Oaks, CA: Sage Publications.

Derogatis, L. R. (2008). Measures of sexual dysfunction and disorders. In J. A. Rush, Jr., M. B. First, & D. Blacker (Eds.), *Handbook of psychiatric measures* (2nd ed., pp. 601–620). Arlington, VA: American Psychiatric Publishing, Inc.

Derogatis, L., & Kourlesis, S. (1981). An approach to evaluation of sexual problems in the cancer patient. *CA A Cancer Journal for Clinicians, 31*(1), 46–50.

deVillers, L., & Turgeon, H. (2005). The uses and benefits of "sensate focus" exercises. *Contemporary Sexuality, 39,* i-vi.

Duhl, B., & Duhl, F. (1981). Integrative family therapy. In A. Gurman & D. Kniskern (Eds.), *Handbook of family therapy* (pp. 483–516). New York: Brunner/Mazel.

Duncan, B., & Parks, M. (1988). Integrating individual and systems approaches: Strategic behavioral therapy. *Journal of Marital and Family Therapy, 14,* 151–162.

Estronaut (1999). A new way to reach orgasm: CAT. Retrieved May 20, 2008 from http://www.womenshealth.org/a/coital_align_technique.htm

Fisher, E. H. (1989). Gender bias in therapy? An analysis of patient and therapist causal explanations. *Psychotherapy: Theory, Research, Practice, Training, 26*(3), 389–401.

Gambescia, N., & Weeks, G. (2007). Sexual dysfunction. In N. Kazantzis & L. L'Abate (Eds.), *Handbook of homework assignments in psychotherapy: Research, practice, prevention* (pp. 351–368). New York: Springer Science + Business Media.

Gill, K. M., & Hough, S. (2007). Sexuality training, education and therapy in the healthcare environment: Taboo, avoidance, discomfort or ignorance? *Sexuality and Disability, 25,* 73-76.

Gott, M. (2004). *Sexuality, sexual health and ageing.* Buckingham: Open University Press.

Gott, M. (2006). Sexual health and the new ageing. *Age and Ageing, 35,* 106–107.

Gottman, J. M. (1994). *What predicts divorce? The relationship between marital process and marital outcomes.* Hillsdale, NJ: Lawrence Erlbaum Associates.

Guanipa, C., & Woolley, S. R. (2000). Gender biases and therapists' conceptualization of couple difficulties. *American Journal of Family Therapy, 28*(2), 181–192.

Gudjonsson, G. H. (1986). Sexual variations: Assessment and treatment in clinical practice. *Sexual and Marital Therapy, 1*(2), 191–214.

Gurman, A. S., & Fraenkel, P. (2002). The history of couple therapy: A millennial review. *Family Process, 41*(2), 199–260.

Handy, L., Valentich, M., Cammaert, L., & Gripton, J. (1985). Feminist issues in sex therapy. *Feminist Perspectives on Social Work and Human Sexuality, 3,* 69–80.

Harbison, J. J. M., Graham, P. J., Quinn, J. T., McAllister, H., & Woodward, R. (1974). A questionnaire measure of sexual interest. *Archives of Sexual Behavior, 3*(4), 357–366.

Hartman, W. E., & Fithian, M. A. (1972). *Treatment of sexual dysfunction: A biopsycho-social approach* (1st ed.). Long Beach, CA: Center for Marital & Sexual Studies.

Hatcher, C. (1978). Intrapersonal and interpersonal models: Blending Gestalt and family therapies. *Journal of Marriage and Family Counseling, 4,* 63–68.

Hecker, L. L., Trepper, T. S., Wetchler, J. L., & Fontaine, K. L. (1995) The influence of therapist values, religiosity and gender in the initial assessment of sexual addiction by family therapists. *American Journal of Family Therapy, 23*(3), 261–272.

Heiman, J. R. (2002). Psychologic treatments for female sexual dysfunction: Are they effective and do we need them? *Archives of Sexual Behavior, 31*(5), 445–450.

Heiman, J., LoPiccolo, J., & Palladini, D. (1988). *Becoming orgasmic: A sexual and personal growth program for women.* New York: Prentice Hall Press.

Hertlein, K. M. (2004). *Internet infidelity: An examination of family therapist treatment decisions and gender biases.* Unpublished doctoral dissertation. Virginia Tech.

Hertlein, K. M., Weeks, G. R., & Gambescia, N. (2008). *Systemic sex therapy.* New York: Taylor & Francis.

Hill, D., & Coll, H. (1992). Ethical issues in marital and sexual counseling. *British Journal of Guidance & Counseling, 20,* 75–89.

Hof, L., & Berman, E. (1986). The sexual genogram. *Journal of Marital and Family Therapy, 12*(1), 39–47.

Hollows, K. (2007). Anodyspareunia: A novel sexual dysfunction? An exploration into anal sexuality. *Sexual and Relationship Therapy, 22*(4), 429–443.

Hoon, E. F., Hoon, P. W., & Wincze, J. P. (1976). An inventory for the measure of female sexual arousability: The SAI. *Archives of Sexual Behavior, 5*(4), 291–300.

Hoon, P. W., Wincze, J. P., & Hoon, E. F. (1976). Physiological assessment of sexual arousal in women. *Psychophysiology, 13*(3), 196–204.

Hulter, B., & Lundberg, P. (1995). Sexual function in women with advanced multiple sclerosis. *Journal of Neurological and Neurosurgery Psychiatry, 59,* 83–86.

Kahn, A. L., Whipple, B., & Perry, J. D. (1982). *The G spot.* New York: Atcom Publishing.

Kalayjian, L., & Morrell, M. (2000). Female sexuality and neurological disease. *Journal of Sex Education and Therapy, 25*(1), 89–95.

Kaplan, H. S. (1974). *The new sex therapy.* New York: Brunner/Mazel.

Kaplan, H. S. (1992) Does the CAT technique enhance female orgasm? *Journal of Sex and Marital Therapy, 18*(4), 285–291.

Kimmel, M. (2007). *The sexual self: The construction of sexual scripts.* Nashville, TN: Vanderbilt University Press.

Kinzl, J., Mangweth, B., Traweger, C., & Beible, W. (1996). Sexual dysfunction in males: Significance of adverse childhood experiences. *Child Abuse and Neglect, 20,* 759–766.

Kinzl, J., Traweger, C., & Beibl, W. (1995). Sexual dysfunctions: Relationship to childhood sexual abuse and early family experiences in a nonclinical sample. *Child Abuse and Neglect, 19,* 785–792.

Klein, M. (1997). Disorders of desire. In R. Charlton (Ed.), *Treating sexual disorders* (pp. 201–236). San Francisco: Jossey–Bass.

Komisaruk, B. R., Beyer-Flores, C., & Whipple, B. (2006). *The science of orgasm.* Baltimore, MD: John Hopkins University Press.

Koukounas, E., & McCabe, M. P. (2001). Sexual and emotional variables influencing sexual response to erotica: A psychophysiological investigation. *Archives of Sexual Behavior, 30*(4), 393–408.

L'Abate, L. (2007). *Low-cost interventions to promote physical and mental health: Theory, research, and practice.* New York: Springer.

Laumann, E., Nicolosi, A., Glasser, D., Paik, A., Gingell, C., Moreira, E., et al. (2005). Sexual problems among women and men aged 40–80 years: Prevalence and correlates identified in the Global Study of Sexual Attitudes and Behaviors. *International Journal of Impotence Research, 17*(1), 39–57.

Laumann, E. O., Paik, A., & Rosen, R. C. (1999). Sexual dysfunction in the United States: Prevelance and predictors. *Journal of the American Medical Association, 281*(6), 537–544.

Leiblum, S. R. (2008). *Principles and practice of sex therapy* (4th ed.). New York: Guilford Press.

Leiblum, S. R. (2007a). Sex therapy today: Current issues and future perspectives. In S. R. Leiblum (Ed.), *Principles and practice of sex therapy* (4th ed., pp. 3–22). New York: Guilford Press.

Leiblum, S. R. (2007b). Persistent genital arousal disorder: Perplexing, distressing and under-recognized. In S. R. Leiblum (Ed.), *Principles and practice of sex therapy* (4th ed., pp. 54–83). New York: Guilford Press.

Leiblum, S. R., & Rosen, R. C. (Eds.). (1988). *Sexual desire disorders.* New York: Guilford Press.

Leiblum, S. R., & Rosen, R. C. (Eds.). (1989). *Principles and practice of sex therapy: Updated for the 1990s* (2nd ed.). New York: Guilford Press.

Letourneau, E. J. (2002). A comparison of objective measures of sexual arousal and interest: Visual reaction time and penile plethysmography. *Sexual Abuse: Journal of Research and Treatment, 14*(3), 207–223.

Lewis, R. W., Fugl-Meyer, K. S., Bosch, R., Fugl-Meyer, A. R., Laumann, E. O., Lizza, E., & Martin-Morales, A. (2004). Epidemiology/risk factors of sexual dysfunction. *Journal of Sexual Medicine 1*(1), 35–39.

Liss-Levinson, N. (1979). Women with sexual concerns. *Counseling Psychologist, 8*(1), 36–37.

LoPiccolo, J., & Steger, J. (1974). The sexual interaction inventory: A new instrument for assessment of sexual dysfunction. *Archives of Sexual Behavior, 3,* 585–595.

Loren, R. E., & Weeks, G. R. (1986). Sexual fantasies of undergraduates and their perceptions of the sexual fantasies of the opposite sex. *Journal of Sex Education & Therapy, 12*(2), 31–36.

Mah, K., & Binik, Y. M. (2002). Do all orgasms feel alike? Evaluating a two-dimensional model of the orgasm experience across gender and sexual context. *Journal of Sex Research, 39*(2), 104–113.

Marks, I. M., & Sartorius, N. H. (1967). A contribution to the measurement of sexual attitude. *Journal of Nervous and Mental Disease, 145*(6), 441–451.

Masters, W. H., & Johnson, V. E. (1966). *Human sexual response.* Boston: Little, Brown.

Masters, W. H., & Johnson, V. (1970). *Human sexual inadequacy.* Boston: Little, Brown.

McCabe, M. P. (1994). The influence of the quality of relationship on sexual dysfunction. *Australian Journal of Marriage and Family, 15,* 2–8.

McCarthy, B. W. (1985). Use and misuse of behavioral homework exercises in sex therapy. *Journal of Sex and Marital Therapy, 11*(3), 185–191.

McCarthy, B., & Fucito, L. (2005). Integrating medication, realistic expectations and therapeutic interventions in the treatment of male sexual dysfunction. *Journal of Sex & Marital Therapy, 31,* 319–328.

McCoy, N. L., & Matyas, J. R. (1998). McCoy female sexuality questionnaire. In C. M. Davis, W. L. Yarber, R. Bauserman, G. Schreer, & S. L. Davis (Eds.), *Handbook of sexuality related measures* (pp. 249–251). Thousand Oaks, CA: Sage Publications.

McGoldrick, M., & Gerson, R. (1985). *Genograms in family assessment.* New York: Norton.

McGoldick, M., Gerson, R., & Shellenberger, S. (1999). *Genograms: Assessment and intervention* (2nd ed.). New York: W. W. Norton & Co.

Meana, M., Binik, Y. M., & Thaler, L. (2006). Assessment of sexual dysfunction. In J. Hunsley & E. J. Mash (Eds.), *A guide to assessments that work* (pp. 1–61). New York: Oxford University Press.

Metz, M. E., & Epstein, N. (2002). Assessing the role of relationship conflict in sexual dysfunction. *Journal of Sex and Marital Therapy, 28*(2), 139–164.

Mezzich, J., & Hernandez-Serrano, R. (2006). *Psychiatry and sexual health: An integrative approach.* Lanham, MD: World Psychiatric Association.

Michael, R. T., Gagnon, J. H., Laumann, E. O., & Kolata, G. (1994). *Sex in America: A definitive survey.* New York: Warner Books, Inc.

Money, J. (1986). *Lovemaps: Clinical concepts of sexual/erotic health and pathology, paraphilia, and gender transposition in childhood, adolescence, and maturity.* New York: Irvington Publishers.

Mosher, D. L. (1979). Sex guilt and sex myths in college men and women. *Journal of Sex Research, 15*(3), 224–234.

Nijs, P. (2006). Mental health of sex counselors and of sex therapists: Some guidelines. *Sexual and Relationship Therapy, 21,* 124–129.

O'Leary, M. P., Fowler, F. J., Lenderking, W. R., Barber, B., Sagnier, P. P., Guess, H. A., et al. (1995). A brief male sexual function inventory for urology. *Urology, 46,* 697–706.

Paitich, D., Langevin, R., Freeman, R., Mann, K., & Handy, L. (1977). The Clarke SHQ: A clinical sex history questionnaire for males. *Archives of Sexual Behavior, 6*(5), 421–436.

Panchana, N. A., & Sofronoff, K. (2005). Sexual problems. In N. Kazantzis, F. P. Deane, K. R. Ronan, & L. L'Abate (Eds.), *Using homework assignments in cognitive behavior therapy* (pp. 307–327). New York: Routledge/Taylor & Francis Group.

Pangman, V. C., & Seguire, M. (2000). Sexuality and the chronically ill older adult: A social justice issue. *Sexuality and Disability, 18*(1), 49–59.

Peterson, F. L. (2007). The complexity of sexual diversity: Sexual identity cube and self-awareness exercise. In L. VandeCreek, F. L. Peterson, & J. W. Bley (Eds.), *Innovations in clinical practice: Focus on sexual health* (pp. 297–300). Sarasota, FL: Professional Resource Press/Professional Resource Exchange.

Peterson, F. L., & Peterson, C. C. (2007). A healthcare professional's guide to contemporary sexual myths. In L. VandeCreek, F. L. Peterson, & J. W. Bley (Eds.), *Innovations in clinical practice: Focus on sexual health* (pp. 323–326). Sarasota, FL: Professional Resource Press/Professional Resource exchange.

Physicians' desk reference (56th ed.). (2002). Montvale, NJ: Medical Economics Company.

Pinsof, W. (1992). Toward a scientific paradigm for family therapy. *Journal of Family Psychology, 5,* 432–447.

Pion, R. J., & Wagner, N. N. (1971). Diagnosis and treatment of inadequate sexual responses. In J. J. Rovinsky (Ed.), *Davis' gynecology and obstetrics* (pp. 1–17). Hagerstown, MD: Harper & Row.

Plaud, J., Dubbert, P., Holm, J., Wittrock, D., Smith, P., Edison, J., et al. (1996). Erectile dysfunction in men with chronic medical illness. *Journal of Behavior Therapy and Experimental Psychology, 27,* 11–19.

Podell, L., & Perkins, J. C. (1957). A Guttman scale for sexual experience: A methodological note. *The Journal of Abnormal and Social Psychology, 54*(3), 420–422.

Porst, H., & Buvat, J. (2003). *Standard practice in sexual medicine.* Malden, MA: Blackwell Publishing.

Quinsey, V. L., Steinman, C. M., Bergersen, S. G., & Holmes, T. F. (1975). Penile circumference, skin conductance, and ranking responses of child molesters and "normals" to sexual and nonsexual visual stimuli. *Behavior Therapy, 6*(2), 213–219.

Quirk, F. H., Haughie, S., & Symonds, T. (2005). The use of the sexual function questionnaire as a screening tool for women with sexual dysfunction. *Journal of Sexual Medicine, 2,* 469–477.

Quirk, F. H., Heiman, J. R., & Rosen, R. C. (2002). Development of sexual function questionnaire for clinical trials of female sexual dysfunction. *Journal of Women's Health & Gender-Based Medicine, 11*(3), 277–289.

Ravella, D. (2007). Ethics in sex therapy. In L. Vandecreek, F. Peterson, Jr., & J. Bley (Eds.), *Innovations in clinical practice: Focus on sexual health* (pp. 63–72). Sarasota, FL: Professional Resource Press.

Redlich, F. (1980). The ethics of sex therapy. In W. H. Masters, V. E. Johnson, & R. C. Kolodny (Eds.), *Ethical issues in sex therapy and research* (pp. 143–181). Boston: Little Brown and Company.

Riegel, K. (1976). The dialectics of human development. *American Psychologist, 31*, 689–700.

Rieker, P. P., & Carmen, E. H. (1983). Teaching value clarification: The example of gender and psychotherapy. *American Journal of Psychiatry, 140*(4), 410–415.

Riley, A. (1991). Sexuality and the menopause. *Sexual and Marital Therapy, 6*, 135–146.

Rockliffe-Fidler, C., & Kiemle, G. (2003). Sexual function in diabetic women: A psychological perspective. *Sexual and Relationship Therapy, 18*(2), 143–159.

Rogers, G. S., Van de Castle, R. L., Evans, W. S., & Critelli, J. W. (1985). Vaginal pulse amplitude response patterns during erotic conditions and sleep. *Archives of Sexual Behavior, 14*(4), 327–342.

Rosen, R. (2007). Erectile dysfunction: Integration of medical and psychological approaches. In S. R. Leiblum (Ed.), *Principles and practice of sex therapy* (4th ed., pp. 277–310). New York: Guilford Press.

Rosen, R., Brown, C., Heiman, J., Leiblum, S., Meston, C., Shabsigh, R. et al. (2000). The female sexual function index (FSFI): A multidimensional self-report instrument for the assessment of female sexual function. *Journal of Sex and Marital Therapy, 26*, 191–208.

Rosen, R. C., Lobo, R. A., Block, B. A., Yang, H-M., & Zipfel, L. M. (2004). Menopausal sexual interest questionnaire (MSIQ): A unidimensional scale for the assessment of sexual interest in postmenopausal women. *Journal of Sex and Marital Therapy, 30*, 235–250.

Rosen, R. C., Riley, A., Wagner, G., Osterloh, I. H., Kirkpatrick, J., & Mishra, A. (1997). The international index of erectile function (IIEF): A multidimensional scale for assessment of erectile dysfunction. *Urology, 49*, 822–830.

Rosen, R. C., Taylor, J. E., & Leiblum, S. (1998). Brief index of sexual functioning for women. In C. M. Davis, W. L. Yarber, R. Bauserman, G. Schreer, & S. L. Davis (Eds.), *Handbook of sexuality-related measures* (pp. 251–255). Thousand Oaks, CA: Sage Publications.

Rosen, R. C., Leiblum, S. R., & Spector, I. (1994). Psychologically-based treatment for male erectile disorder: A cognitive-interpersonal model. *Journal of Sex & Marital Therapy, 20*, 67-85.

Rosser, B. R. S., Short, B. J., Thurmes, P. J., & Coleman, E. (1998). Anodyspareunia, the unacknowledged sexual dysfunction: A validation study of painful receptive anal intercourse and its psychosexual concomitants in homosexual men. *Journal of Sex and Marital Therapy, 24*, 281–292.

Rust, J., & Golombok, S. (1985). The Golombok–Rust inventory of sexual satisfaction (GRISS). *British Journal of Clinical Psychology, 24*(1), 63–64.

Rust, J., & Golombok, S. (1986). The GRISS: A psychometric instrument for the assessment of sexual dysfunction. *Archives of Sexual Behavior, 15*, 153–165.

Rust, J., & Golombok, S. (1998). The GRISS: A psychometric scale and profile of sexual dysfunction. In C. M. Davis, W. L. Yarber, R. Bauserman, G. Schreer, & S. L. Davis (Eds.), *Handbook of sexuality-related measures* (pp. 192–194). Thousand Oaks, CA: Sage Publications.

Schiavi, R. C. (1992). Laboratory methods for evaluating erectile dysfunction. In R. C. Rosen & S. R. Leiblum (Eds.), *Erectile disorders: Assessment and treatment* (pp. 141–170). New York: Guilford Press.

Schiavi, R. C., Derogatis, L. R., Kuriansky, J., O'Connor, D., & Sharpe, L. (1979). The assessment of sexual function and marital interaction. *Journal of Sex and Marital Therapy, 5*(3), 169–224.

Schiavi, R. C., Stimmel, B. B., Mandeli, J., Schreiner-Engel, P., & Ghizzani, A. (1995). Diabetes, psychological function and male sexuality. *Journal of Psychosomatic Research, 39*, 305–314.

Schneider, J., & Levinson, B. (2006). Ethical dilemmas related to disclosure issues: Sex addiction therapists in the trenches. *Journal of Sexual Addiction and Compulsivity, 13*, 1–39.

Schover, L. R. (1981). Male and female therapists' responses to male and female client sexual material: An analogue study. *Archives of Sexual Behavior, 10*(6), 477–492.

Schwartz, P., & Strom, D. (1978). The social psychology of female sexuality. In J. A. Sherman & F. L. Denmark (Eds.), *The psychology of women: Future directions in research*. New York: WES-DEN.

Seagraves, R., & Balon, R. (2003). *Sexual pharmacology: Fast facts*. New York: W. W. Norton.

Seidman, S. N., & Roose, S. P. (2000). The relationship between depression and erectile dysfunction. *Current Psychiatry Reports, 2*, 201–205.

Sherman, J. (1980). Mathematics, spatial visualization, and related factors: Changes in girls and boys, grades 8–11. *Journal of Educational Psychology, 72*(4), 476–482.

Sherman, J. A. (1982). Mathematics the critical filter: A look at some residues. *Psychology of Women Quarterly, 6*(4), 428–444.

Simon, W. T., & Schouten, P. G. (1991). Plethysmography in the assessment and treatment of sexual deviance: An overview. *Archives of Sexual Behavior, 20*(1), 75–91.

Sipski, M. L., & Alexander, C. J. (Eds.). (1997). *Sexual function in people with disability and chronic illness: A health professional's guide*. Gaithersburg, MD: Aspen Publishers.

Slife, B., & Reber, J. (2001). Eclecticism in psychotherapy: Is it really the best substitute for traditional theories? In B. Slife, R.Williams, & S. Barlow (Eds.), *Critical issues in psychotherapy: Translating new ideas into practice* (pp. 213–233). Thousand Oaks, CA: Sage Publications.

Smith, D., Carvalhal, G., Schneider, K., Krygiel, J., Yan, Y., & Catalona, W. (2000). Quality-of-life outcomes for men with prostate carcinoma detected by screening. *Cancer, 88*(6), 1454–1463.

Society for the Scientific Study of Sexuality. (2007). *Ethics statement*. Retrieved May 24, 2008 from: http://www.sexscience.org/about/index.php?category_id=162

Soler, J. M., Previnaire, J. G., Denys, P., & Chartier-Kastler, E. (2007). Phosphodiesterase inhibitors in the treatment of erectile dysfunction in spinal cord-injured men. *Spinal Cord, 45*(2), 169–173.

Spector, I. P., Leiblum, S. R., Carey, M. P., & Rosen, R. C. (1993). Diabetes and sexual function: A critical review. *Annals of Behavioral Medicine, 15,* 257–264.

Sternberg, R. (1986). A triangular theory of love. *Psychological Review, 93,* 119–135.

Stewart, E. G., & Spencer, P. (2002) *The V book: A doctor's guide to complete vulvovaginal health.* New York: Bantam Books.

Strong, S., & Claiborn, C. (1982). *Change through interaction: Social psychological processes of counseling and psychotherapy.* New York: Wiley.

Sugrue, D. P., & Whipple, B. (2001). The consensus-based classification of female sexual dysfunction: Barriers to universal acceptance. *Journal of Sex and Marital Therapy, 27*(2), 221–226.

Talmadge, L. D., & Talmadge, W. C. (1990). Sexuality assessment measures for clinical use: A review. *American Journal of Family Therapy, 18*(1), 80–105.

Taylor, J. F., Rosen, R. C., & Leiblum, S. R. (1994). Self-report assessment of female sexual function: Psychometric evaluation of the brief index of sexual functioning for women. *Archives of Sexual Behavior, 23*(6), 627–643.

Tepper, B. J. (2000). Consequences of abusive supervision. *Academy of Management Journal, 43,* 178–190.

Tepper, M. S. (1997). Providing comprehensive sexual health care in spinal cord injury rehabilitation: Implementation and evaluation of a new curriculum for health care professionals. *Sexuality and Disability, 15*(3), 131–165.

Tepper, M. S. (2000). Sexuality and disability: The missing discourse of pleasure. *Sexuality and Disability, 18*(4), 283–290.

Thomas, A. J. (1998). Understanding culture and worldview in family systems: Use of a multicultural genogram. *The Family Journal, 6*(1), 24–32.

Thorne, F. C. (1966a). The sex inventory. *Journal of Clinical Psychology, 22,* 367–374.

Thorne, F. C. (1966b). A factorial study of sexuality in adult males. *Journal of Clinical Psychology, 22,* 378–386.

Tiefer, L. (2001). New view of women's sexual problems: Why new? Why now? *Journal of Sex Research, 38,* 89–96.

Tiefer, L. (2002). Beyond the medical model of women's sexual problems: A campaign to resist the promotion of "female sexual dysfunction." *Sexual and Relationship Therapy, 17*(2), 127–135.

Tompkins, M. A. (2004). *Using homework in psychotherapy.* New York: Guilford Press.

Træen, B., & Olsen, S. (2007). Sexual dysfunction and sexual well-being in people with heart disease. *Sexual and Relationship Therapy, 22*(2), 193–208.

Trepper, T., Treyger, S., Yalowitz, J., & Ford, J. (2008). Solution-focused brief therapy for the treatment of sexual disorders. In K. Hertlein, G. Weeks, & N. Gambescia (Eds.), *Systemic sex therapy.* New York: Taylor & Francis.

Turner, M. (2008). Uncovering and treating sex addiction in couples. In K. Hertlein, G. Weeks, & N. Gambescia (Eds.), *Systemic sex therapy.* New York: Taylor & Francis.

Underwood, S. G. (2003). Gay men and anal eroticism: Tops, bottoms and versatiles. New York: The Haworth Press Inc.

Utian, W. H., McLean, D. B., Symonds, T., Symons, J., Somayaji, V., & Sisson, M. (2005). A methodology study to validate a structured diagnostic method used to diagnose female sexual dysfunction and its subtypes in postmenopausal women. *Journal of Sex and Marital Therapy, 31,* 271–283.

Valentich, M., & Gripton, J. (1984). Facilitating the sexual integration of the head-injured person in the community. *Sexuality and Disability, 7*(1–2), 28–42.

VandeCreek, L., Peterson, F. L., Jr., & Bley, J. W. (Eds.). (2007). *Innovations in clinical practice: Focus on sexual health.* Sarasota, FL: Professional Resource Press/Professional Resource exchange.

Van Kaam, A. (1969). *Existential foundations of psychology.* New York: Basic Books.

Wakefield, J. C. (1987). Sex bias in the diagnosis of primary orgasmic dysfunction. *American Psychologist, 42*(5), 464–471.

Weeks, G. (1977). Toward a dialectical approach to intervention. *Human Development, 20,* 277–292.

Weeks, G. (Ed.). (1985). *Promoting change through paradoxical therapy.* Homewood, IL: Dow Jones.

Weeks, G. (1986). Individual system dialectic. *American Journal of Family Therapy, 14,* 5–12.

Weeks, G. (1989). *Treating couples: The intersystem model of the Marriage Council of Philadelphia.* New York: Brunner/Mazel.

Weeks, G. (1994). The Intersystem model: An integrative approach to treatment. In Weeks, G., & Hof, L. (Eds.), *The marital-relationship therapy casebook: Theory and application of the intersystem model* (pp. 3–34). New York: Brunner/Mazel.

Weeks, G., & Gambescia, N. (2000). *Erectile dysfunction: Integrating couple therapy, sex therapy, and medical treatment.* New York: W. W. Norton.

Weeks, G., & Gambescia, N. (2002). *Hypoactive sexual desire: Integrating couple and sex therapy.* New York: W. W. Norton.

Weeks, G., Gambescia, N., & Jenkins, R. (2003). *Treating infidelity.* New York: W. W. Norton.

Weeks, G., & Hof, L. (Eds.) (1987). *Integrating sex and marital therapy: A clinical guide.* New York: W. W. Norton.

Weeks, G. R., & Hof, L. (1994). *The marital-relationship therapy casebook: Theory and application of the Intersystem model.* Philadelphia, PA: Brunner/Mazel.

Weeks, G. R., Odell, M., & Methven, S. (2005). *If only I had known: Avoiding common mistakes in couples therapy.* New York: W. W. Norton & Co.

Weeks, G., & Treat, S. (1992). *Couples in treatment: Techniques and approaches for effective practice.* Philadelphia, PA: Brunner/Mazel.

Weeks, G., & Treat, S. (2001a). *Couples in treatment* (Rev. ed.). New York: Brunner/Routledge.

Weeks, G., & Treat, S. (2001b). *Couples in treatment: Techniques and approaches for effective practice* (2nd ed.). Philadelphia, PA: Brunner/Routledge.

Westfall, A. (2000). The intersystem model. In F. M. Dattilio & L. J. Bevilacqua (Eds.), *Comparative treatments for relationship dysfunction* (pp. 229–246). New York: Springer.

Whipple, B., & Komisaruk, B. (2002). Brain (PET) responses to vaginal–cervical self-stimulation in women with complete spinal cord injury: Preliminary findings. *Journal of Sex & Marital Therapy, 28*(1), 79–86.

Whitley, M. P. (1974). *A correlational survey comparing the levels of assertiveness with levels of sexual satisfaction in employed sexually active professional women.* Unpublished master's thesis, University of Washington, Seattle.

Williams, K. M. (2003). Two techniques for assessment of sexual interest: A discussion of the clinical utility of *penile plethysmography* and visual reaction time. *The Forensic Examiner, 12*(1–2), 35–38.

Wincze, J. P., & Carey, M. P. (2001). *Sexual dysfunction: A guide for assessment and treatment* (2nd ed.). New York: Guilford Press.

Zilbergeld, B. (1992). *The new male sexuality.* New York: Bantam Books.

Zuckerman, M. (1973). Scales for sex experience for males and females. *Journal of Consulting and Clinical Psychology, 41*(1), 27–29.

Zuckerman, M., Tushup, R., & Finner, S. (1976). Sexual attitudes and experience: Attitude and personality correlates and changes produced by a course in sexuality. *Journal of Consulting and Clinical Psychology, 44*(1), 7–19.

Zygmond, M. J., & Denton, W. (1988). Gender bias in marital therapy: A multidimensional scaling analysis. *American Journal of Family Therapy, 16*(3), 262–272.

Index